Hippocrene U.S.A. Guide to
HISTORIC BLACK SOUTH

Hippocrene U.S.A. Guide to

HISTORIC BLACK SOUTH

Historical Sites, Cultural Centers, and Musical Happenings of the African-American South

Jim Haskins & Joann Biondi

HIPPOCRENE BOOKS
New York

Acknowledgments

The authors are grateful to Kathy Benson, Deidre Grafel, Ann Kalkhoff, and Louise Stephenson for their help.

For information, address
HIPPOCRENE BOOKS, INC.
171 Madison Ave.
New York, NY 10016

Library of Congress Cataloging in Publication Data
Haskins, James, 1941-
    Hippocrene U.S.A. guide to historic Black South :
historical sites, cultural centers, and musical happenings
of the African-American South / Jim haskins & Joann
Biondi.
        p. cm.
    Includes index.
    ISBN 0-7818-0140-0 :
    1. Afro-Americans—Southern States—History. 2.
Historic sites-Southern States—Guidebooks. 3. southern
states—Guidebooks.
    I. Biondi, Joann. II. Title. II. Title: Hippocrene U.S.A.
guide to historic Black South. IV. Title: Historic Black
South.
E185.92.H38 1993   93-18334
975'.00496073—dc20   CIP

Printed in the United States of America

To Deidre

Contents

Oh, the places you will go
—Dr. Seuss

Introduction

Most of the historic sites and vibrant cultural centers of America's black South have been woefully ignored by the mainstream, travel-writing press. Guidebooks on the area tend to accent post-card-perfect attractions of conventional appeal while leaving out the very segment of the South that is crucial to understanding its unique personality. It is only recently that state tourist boards have begun to include references to the black heritage of their areas in promotional materials.

Although desegregation has been accomplished in theory, for the most part, black neighborhoods, in the South and in the North, have remained self-contained and separate entities unto themselves. Despite poor economic conditions, these communities are often full of rich authenticity and a spirited sense of place, two things that are slowly vanishing from the homogenized American landscape. For many American whites, these black neighborhoods have long been off-limits because they were deemed "unsafe." But recent trends show that more and more Americans, and travelers from abroad, want to experience the down-home nuances of the black communities, and are seeking out the varied ethnic encounters that the United States has to offer.

As a destination, the South evokes an array of images: great plantation houses and sparse slave cabins, mint juleps and Jack Daniels, Blanche DuBois and Uncle Remus, red clay and "The Color Purple." It is full of Dixie pride and slow Southern drawl. Forgotten in the North, the Civil War remains a wound in the South, an historical trauma that represents a tragic loss to some and an ebullient gain to others.

The black South, an area chock-full of historical and cultural landmarks of African-American significance, should not be considered just an offbeat, road-less-traveled section of the more traditional South, but the foundation of its very existence. For in the early years it was the black population that paved most of the streets, constructed most of the buildings, and tended to the crops that brought wealth to the region.

Before the civil rights movement transformed the social conscience of this country, blacks who traveled through the South faced racism at its harshest. Just 30 years ago, blacks could not rent a highway motel room or order coffee at a small-town cafe. Neither could they use a public toilet or drink from a "whites only" water-fountain. But fortunately, the region that once said "never" to racial desegregation has changed. The so-called New South of today is as much about big-city sophistication as it is about ripe roadside peaches. It is also about great museums, great music, great restaurants, and great people, in both white and black communities.

Throughout the South there are individuals and organizations committed to preserving black historic sites so that they don't disappear and become lost forever. The resources needed to accomplish this task are scarce, and the fact that many of these sites are still standing at all is truly remarkable. Holding on to our heritage is a difficult job.

Introduction

The compilation in this book includes historic sites, churches, museums, art galleries, festivals, restaurants, nightclubs, jazz joints, birthplaces, gravesites, radio programs, record stores, barbershops, beaches, parks, schools, and markets—the essence of the black communities.

Some of them are well known and embedded in the American psyche— like the Edmund Pettus Bridge in Selma, Alabama, where civil rights marchers were confronted by police in 1965; or the Lorraine Motel in Memphis, Tennessee site of the assassination of Martin Luther King, Jr., in 1968. Others are more obscure—like the tiny Delta Blues Museum in Clarksdale, Mississippi, or the childhood home of the late Alex Haley in Henning, Tennessee. More than one of the churches listed boasts of being the "first" or the "oldest" of its kind—who wants to argue with a church? A small number of the sites have been abandoned and lie in a sad shambles; some are perfectly preserved. As a collection, they represent the significant contribution that Southern blacks have made to their country.

The purpose of this book is to document and highlight these various contributions and bring them into the forefront where they belong. Each chapter includes a brief synopsis of the black history of that particular state, followed by a series of listings arranged alphabetically within cities. When applicable, hours of operation and phone numbers are listed. Although not individually noted, many of the public sites are closed during federal holidays. Since operating hours often change with time, it is suggested that you phone ahead. Tour companies that specialize in African-American itineraries are also included.

For the curious traveler, this book will serve as a guide

to welcome detours and alternative stops. It will lead you to places otherwise unnoticed, where you can explore at your leisure and get in touch with the past. It is a journey into the soul of the American black South.

Jim Haskins and Joann Biondi
May 1993

African-Americans and the South

What would the South be without African-Americans? What would African-Americans be without the South? For centuries the South was a place where blacks and whites were separate, yet one. As Eugene D. Genovese put it, "As in a lasting, although not necessarily happy marriage, two discrete individuals shared, for better or worse, one life." Whites, enjoying all the political, social, and economic power, imposed some aspects of their culture on blacks while denying them other aspects. They "missionized" them but denied them the opportunity to learn to read. In the meantime, largely out of self interest and often unconsciously, they imbibed much of slave sensibility and culture. They allowed slaves to sing, believing that they were happier and better workers for it, and at the same time felt the beat and the lyrics in their own souls. As the years passed, a distinctive Southern culture emerged, owing much of its uniqueness to both races.

Not until recent years, however, have the contributions of African-Americans been fully acknowledged, and because of the scores of years previously when African-American influence on Southern life was denied, much has been lost, some irretrievably.

The South was the crucible of African-American culture. For nearly 300 years, Africans and the generations they spawned lived in sufficient numbers to create new African-American lifeways. Although the latter half of the twentieth century has seen a wave of migration to Northern urban centers, few Northern blacks are more than a generation removed from the South, and many celebrate, somewhat romantically, the sense of family and communtiy they have been unable to replicate in the North.

The South is not a single entity, nor is the African-American culture that was created in it. After all, slaves were drawn from a region of Africa roughly equal in size to the United States. Moreover, contact between slaves and Native Americans has yet to be studied in depth, though in some areas, perhaps many, it was considerable. In fact, the diversity of the slaves' origins, the variations in Southern history, and the amount of contact among whites, African-Americans, and Native Americans precludes initial generalizations about the relationship between African-Americans and the South.

In the Spanish outpost of St. Augustine, Florida, Native Americans were the majority population, for the Spanish were not interested in settlement but in military security for their ships, bound from Mexico, and in Christian missionary work. The African-American poppulation was negligible. After the English colonized Carolina in 1670, the African-American population began to increase, as fugitive slaves made their way southward across the swamps and marshes of coastal Georgia to Florida and freedom. So many escaped slaves had taken up residence around St. Augustine by 1738 that the governor of the Spanish colony set aside land north of the settlement for a town and a fort. Originally named

Gracia Real de Santa Teresa de Mose, the sites are today called Mose and Fort Mose and are among the most significant in African-American archeology.

During the 1830s, after Spain had ceded the Florida territory to the United States, blacks in Florida merged with the local Seminoles to fight against attempts to move them westward. While they were in the end unsuccessful, these mixed-culture resisters fought for years, seriously impeding development of the territory.

The first Europeans to colonize the area comprising present-day Alabama and Louisiana were French fur traders, who gave Louisiana its name and established the territorial government at Mobile before relocating it to New Orleans. When the French and Indian wars, which pitted the French and their Indian allies against the British, went badly for the French, France secretly ceded the area west of the Mississippi to Spain in order to keep it from falling into British hands.

Subsequently, a large influx of French planters and blacks, slave and free, descended on New Orleans, fleeing the revolution in Santo Domingo that resulted in the creation of Haiti. To these blacks from Haiti is credited the introduction of voodoo traditions, which found fertile soil among the blacks of New Orleans. Moreover, the resultant mix of cultures was unique on the North American continent. The term *Creole* may be used to refer to any person of mixed race and culture, but it is most frequently used in describing the population of new Orleans and its environs.

Alabama, first settled by fur traders, passed to the victorious British in 1763 at the end of the French and Indian Wars. The British in turn ceded the territory to the United States twenty years later. By 1824 the heavy British demand for cotton had transformed the local economy, and Alabama had become a huge cotton-growing region, rich in soil as well as in slaves.

While Alabama later gained a reputation as one of the most harshly segregated states, curiously it also spawned black academic excellence. In the 1950s, Dr. Horace Mann Bond, the foremost black educator of his time, investigated the sources of achievement of black professionals. He found that the majority of black Ph.D. holders, physicians and college teachers were descended from fewer than 500 extended families in existence in 1860. He also found that the approximately ten percent of blacks who were free in 1860 dominated the subsequent production of black professionals and intellectuals. In documenting the geographical origins of black professionals and holders of Ph.D. degrees, Bond found that a sustantial number had roots in Alabama and that, of these, an extremely high percentage traced their roots to Perry County and to the so-called Black Belt.

In Georgia, slavery was illegal until 1750. Even after slavery was introduced with Georgia's elevation to a British royal colony, the impenetrable Okefenokee Swamp and the Everglades, as well as the coastal sea islands, provided refuges for escaped slaves, who formed secret runaway (maroon) settlements. Over the next two hundred years, a combination of events created Atlanta, symbol of the New South and the most hospitable Southern city for blacks.

The Carolinas, with their marshes and excellent rice-cultivation potential, saw slavery from the beginning of European settlement. Some scholars speculate that escaped slaves may have started living with local Indians as early as the 1520s (Ferguson, p.20). By 1740 blacks outnumbered whites in South Carolina by nearly two to one, and one-half of that majority had been born in

Africa. Sea islands off the coast, like those of Georgia, served as refuges for maroons. Two of the most famous slave rebellions occurred in South Carolina—the Stone Rebellion of 1739 and that led by Denmark Vesey in 1822.

The most distinct survivals of African culture are found among the Geechee of the South Carolina sea islands. Among these survivals is the Gullah dialect, so distinct that it has been called by some a separate language.

In Virginia, while African slavery began as early as 1619, it grew slowly, and slaves arrived at a rate of only about twenty per year until around 1680. White indentured servants and Native American slaves in significant numbers made up the servant class until tobacco farming took hold. At no time, however, did the population of African-Americans constitute a majority, as in South Carolina. Archeologists studying colono ware, hand-build pottery made by both Native Americans and African-Americans, find far fewer pieces in Virginia than in the regions to the south.

That is not to say, however, that there was not a significant slave and later free black presence in Virginia. Perhaps the most famous slave revolt in American history, led by the country preacher Nat Turner, occurred in Southampton, Virginia. And it was at Harper's Ferry, Virginia, that the white abolitionist John Brown chose to initiate his plans for a massive slave revolt.

Further overviews of individual states' histories are provided later in this guide. Little more need be cited here to show the diversity of influences on modern-day Southern and African-American culture. The point was to provide a sample of the variety, and to show that in spite of it, some generalizations are possible.

In the South as a whole, by 1776 half a million Africans had arrived. They cleared forests, planted crops, and built homes. They harvested crops, reared their masters' children as well as their own, spun cloth, canned fruits and vegetables, smoked meat, built furniture, shoed horses, wrought intricate ironwork, stitched quilts, milled corn, dug canals, and built rice-field banks. Yet not only did their white masters claim ownership of the improved property, as well as ownership of those who had improved it, but both white masters and mistresses referred to the work done by field and household slaves as if they themselves had done it.

The attitude perisisted until well into the twentieth century. The contributions of African-Americans were virtually invisible, not to mention the people themselves.

In eighteenth-century Williamsburg, Virginia, nearly half the people who lived and worked in the town were black. Yet from the 1920s, when Colonial Williamsburg was established with funds from the Rockefeller Foundation, to well into the 1960s, the black inhabitants of the town were all but ignored. The same was true of other major archeological sites in the United States. Attention was paid to Native American culture, although in a distorted fashion and with little or no acknowledgment of the fact that a surprising number of slaves were Indians, but not to African-American culture.

One major by-product of the civil rights and black power movements of the 1950s, 60s, and 70s was the new interest in black culture and black influences on American culture that they spawned. Black studies departments and courses, and revisionist historians of both races, took a new look at both African-Americans and the South and posited a dialectic between black and white Southerners that toppled the monolithic earlier histories and brought about a recognition, at last, of the important influences black Southerners have exerted on the culture of the region, not to mention that of the United States as a whole.

It was black Southern preachers who introduced religion into politics in the twentieth century. Many of the major civil rights leaders who were born in the South, among them Andrew Young, John Lewis, and of course Martin Luther King, Jr., were ministers. There is little question that they and their nonviolent methods of protest influenced the later antiwar activism of such men of the cloth as the Berrigan brothers. Jesse Jackson sought the position as heir to Dr. King, and during two presidential campaigns possessed the most strongly moral voice of all the candidates.

Further, African-American religious songs are another important contribution of Southern African-Americans. These spirituals, or 'sorrow songs' arose from slave worship, but they soon permeated the very fabric of Southern life. Generations of white children were reared on them. Indeed, today there are spiritual societies whose membership is completely white.

Among African-American cultural influences on American life as a whole, music has been the longest recognized and least resisted. Nineteenth-century minstrelsy, which originated as sympathetic mimicry of black plantation entertainers, was the first American entertainment form that looked to native, rather than to European, sources of inspiration. The later forms of jazz and the blues were perhaps less easily aped and thus were denied access to polite society. Not until recent times have these forms been accorded the respect they deserve as America's most important contribution to the world's music. Both owe their existence to Southern African-Americans. Could there have been jazz without Buddy Bolden, Jelly Roll Morton and other black musicians in New Orleans? And blues without W.C. Handy, born in Florence, Alabama.

Black Southerners are also to be credited with much of the folklore that is native to this country. The character of Br'er Rabbit, made so famous by the white Southern writer Joel Chandler Harris, was an African-American creation, a version of the African trickster spirit.

Other influences include foodways. Rice was most likely introduced to America from Africa in the 1690s, and there is no doubt about the importance of the rice-cultivating skills of African slaves in the development of that cash crop in warm, wet, low country areas such as South Carolina. Okra, cowpeas, eggplant, and sesame were brought from Africa. The traditional African diet contained little meat. The African style of cooking vegetables for a long time and flavoring them with small pieces of meat became popular among Southern whites as well, as aficionados of beans and greens of all varieties cooked with ham hocks or fatback will attest.

And then there are crafts, among them pottery, coiled basketry, woodworking, stone masonry, and ironwork, not to mention influences in other crafts that have yet to be discovered. More undoubtedly will be found. There are now scholars and scientists willing to look. The archeology of African America is yet in its infancy, only some thirty years old. In an indirect fashion, it owes much to 'Lady Bird' Johnson.

In 1965, when she was the First Lady of the United States, Mrs. Lyndon Johnson called together the nation's mayors for a conference on beautifying America. Her intention was to get flowers planted along highways, among other attempts at beautification. But the conference also stimulated the mayors to express their concern that many of the nation's historic buildings and sites were being lost to the rapid construction of the late 1950s and early 1960s. Out of the conference came a committee, and a report titled "With Heritage So Rich" that led to the passage in 1966 of the National Historic Preservation Act.

Although neither the report nor the act specifically mentioned African-Americans, Leland Ferguson, associate professor of anthropology at the University of South Carolina, Columbia, and a leading expert in African-American archeology, avers that "the structure of this law, together with the pressure of black social and political protest, changed archeology and turned it toward the greatest single source of data about the history of early African-Americans—their archeological remains."

This guide contains mention of several archeological sites where work is being done. From evidence of house foundations, shards of pottery, and slave burial grounds, a small but growing number of specialists in the field are prying open what was once a closed chapter in American history. It is hoped that more will be discovered.

In the meantime, this guide covers African-American history in the South as it is currently known, including formal and informal landmarks and a variety of testaments to the idea that neither African-Americans nor the American South would be what they are today without the influence of each other.

Even a brief perusal will show readers what the impact of Southern black Americans has been on American history and culture. On literature: folklorist Zora Neale Hurston and James Weldon Johnson, who wrote the

"Black National Anthem" from Florida. On political life: Blanche K. Bruce of South Carolina during Reconstruction, and in our time, Fannie Lou Hamer of Mississippi, who helped change the face of the Democratic Party in 1964, and Virginia's L. Douglas Wilder. On music: William Grant Still, born in Mississippi in 1895, the first black composer to write musical scores for Hollywood movies, and Alabaman James Reese Europe, whose 369th Infantry Band brought jazz to Europe during World War I, and in our time, Wynton and Branford Marsalis of Louisiana.

On technology and science: Louisiana's Norbert Rillieux, whose process for refining sugar revolutionized the sugar industry, Alabama's Dr. Percy Julian, who developed cortisone, and Madam C.J. Walker, born in Louisiana, whose secret process for stimulating hair growth made her the first female self-made millionaire in America.

On art: Romare Bearden, born in North Carolina. On athletics: Jesse Owens, born in Alabama. On education: Marva Collins, born in Alabama. Even such a brief listing gives an idea of the importance of the South not only as a crucible, but also as a cradle, of African-American culture and cultural influences.

ALABAMA

From its earliest days, Alabama has been a battleground, first for French, British, and Spanish forces vying for the lands of the New World and later in the struggle between European settlers and Native Americans. The October 18, 1540, battle between European settlers and the poorly equipped warriors of Chief Tuscaloosa has been described as the bloodiest single encounter between whites and Indians in what was to become the United States.

Alabama was the site of important battles in the Civil War and, nearly a century later, of some of the most significant events in the civil rights struggle.

Alabama's band of prairie lowland known as the Black Belt or Cotton Belt established the state's farm-based economy early on. With the population influx following the Louisiana Purchase that established United States control of the area, and the introduction of Whitney's cotton gin that established cotton as the state's major crop and slavery as the area's most important characteristic, by 1860 Alabama's population reached almost one million, nearly half of which was black. Slavery was considered essential to the state's economic and social well-being.

Alabama seceded from the Union and in 1861 joined the Confederate States of America, which was founded in Montgomery, its first capital. The Montgomery home of President Jefferson Davis is now listed on the National Register of Historic Places.

Following the Confederate defeat, Alabama underwent the same political, economic, and social turmoil that marked the Reconstruction period in other states. But once segregationist forces had succeeded in establishing a Jim Crow social system aimed at controlling its valuable labor force, the boll weevil upset the state's social and economic structure. An exodus of rural Alabamians, mostly black, also forced the state from reliance on the one-crop economy and into diversification.

Those blacks who remained suffered largely in silence until December 1, 1955, when a 42-year-old seamstress named Rosa Parks calmly refused to give up her seat on a Montgomery city bus to a white man. Her resulting arrest sparked the year-long Montgomery bus boycott and elevated to national stature the Reverend Martin Luther King, Jr., who had recently arrived in Montgomery to take up the pastorship of Dexter Avenue Baptist Church.

After the student sit-in movement that began in 1960 ushered the civil rights movement into a new, more confrontational era, Alabama was the scene of many major events in the struggle. In Anniston, Freedom Riders testing a new interstate transportation law were beaten. In Birmingham, bombings of black homes and institutions led to the city's being nicknamed "Bombingham." In Selma, white resistance to a campaign for black voting rights led to the famous Selma-to-Montgomery March in 1965.

Alabama has cradled significant black educational achievement. In the 1950s, the renown black educator Horace Mann Bond (father of Julian Bond) documented the geographical origins of black professionals and holders of Ph.D. degrees throughout the United States. He found that the majority of all black Ph.D. holders, physicians, and college teachers hailed from Alabama and were descended from fewer than 500 extended families in existence in 1860.

Of the many black educational institutions in Alabama, Tuskegee Institute, founded in 1881 by Booker T. Washington, is the most famous. Recognized for agricultural research and extension work, its faculty once included Dr. George Washington Carver, who developed 300 derivative products from peanuts and 118 from sweet potatoes.

ALABAMA SITES

For general travel information, and a free brochure on Alabama's Black Heritage Trail, contact the Alabama Bureau of Tourism and Travel, 532 S. Perry St., Montgomery, AL 36104. (800) 252-2262.

ALBERTA

Freedom Quilting Bee—On Hwy. Wilcox 29, in Wilcox County southwest of Selma. (205) 573-2225. Hours: Mon.-Fri. 8-3. Organized in 1966 as an outgrowth of the civil rights movement, the Freedom Quilting Bee was then one of the few all-black-women's cooperatives in the country. It has since achieved national recognition for its quilts, using designs that come out of a 140-year-old tradition. Visitors may view the quilting factory and purchase quilts.

ATHENS

Coleman Hill—Southwest of courthouse square. Coleman Hill was the site of one of 449 Civil War battles in which black units were engaged.

ANNISTON

Anniston Museum of Natural History—4301 McClellan Blvd. (205) 237-6766. Hours: Tues.-Fri. 9-5, Sat. 10-5, Sun. 1-5. Here more that 100 creatures from the African continent are displayed in authentic natural settings. The museum also displays Egyptian mummies, the nation's original diorama bird collection featuring many extinct and endangered species, changing art exhibits. Picnic area and nature trails.

AUBURN

Ebenezer Missionary Baptist Church—Thach St. and Auburn Ave. (205) 821-2929. This 1870 free black church was organized by Thomas Glenn, a prominent area minister after the Civil War, and is noted for its fine craftsmanship. Services still held.

BESSEMER

Old Bessemer Dunbar School—Between 5th and 6th Aves. and 27th and 28th Sts. In 1923, the Bessemer Colored High School opened to grades one through twelve. Renamed Dunbar High School in 1928, it stayed in operation until 1960.

BIRMINGHAM

A.G. Gardens—1501 5th Ave. North, formerly the A.G. Gaston Motel. In 1963, civil rights marchers formed ranks at the A.G. Gaston Motel, for many years the only first-class lodging for blacks. The Gardens now house elderly and handicapped tenants.

Alabama Penny Savings Bank Building—310 18th St.

North. This building once housed the first black-owned bank in the state (1890) and the second largest black bank in the country. The Alabama Penny Savings Bank financed the construction of homes and churches for thousands of black Birmingham area citizens.

Alabama Sports Hall of Fame—Birmingham Jefferson Civic Center, 1 Civic Center Plaza. (205) 323-6665. Hours: Wed.-Sat. 10-5, Tues. and Sun. 1-5. A museum dedicated to the outstanding careers of many black sports figures such as Joe Louis, Jesse Owens, Hank Aaron, Willie Mays, and Billie Williams. Exhibits include sight-and-sound displays, historic film footage of sporting events, and personal memorabilia of athletes

Birmingham Civil Rights Institute—520 16th St. North, (205) 323-2276. Hours: Mon.-Sat. 9-5. Opened in 1992, the institute is a combination museum, research and education center that honors those who fought for the civil rights movement. Housed in a modern brick building with a two-story rotunda, it includes several galleries that chronicle the history of the civil rights movement, the cell in which Dr. Martin Luther King, Jr., was held under arrest in Birmingham, replicas of "whites only" water fountains and lunch counters, and a multi-media presentation that protrays the sights and sounds of famous speeches, bombings, rallies, and jazz, blues and gospel music.

Birmingham Museum of Art—2000 8th Ave. North. (205) 254-2070. Hours: Tues.-Sat. 10-5, Thurs. 5-9, Sun. 1-6. This museum includes primitive, pre-Columbian, Asian, and Indian works as well as a large collection of African art and artifacts.

City Federation of Women's Clubhouse—551 Jasper Rd. This two-story frame house was built to house orphaned and elderly blacks in 1900. It is now used as a day nursery for underprivileged children.

Civil Rights District—Intersection of 16th St. and 6th Ave. This area was once the scene of some of the darkest hours in Birmingham's struggle for civil rights. A statue of Dr. Martin Luther King, Jr., stands in Kelly-Ingram Park, across the street from the Sixteenth Street Baptist Church.

Dr. A.M. Brown House—319 North 4th Ter. Not open to public. This one-and-a-half story structure was originally owned by the black physician who was the founder of World Health Week. It now houses the Birmingham Art Club.

Fourth Avenue District—1600 to 1800 block of Fourth Ave. North and parts of the 300 blocks of 17th and 18th Sts. North. The district is the only surviving remnant of what once was the heart of black Birmingham's social and cultural life and commercial activity during the early twentieth century.

Jazz Hall of Fame Induction Concert—An annual jazz festival held each October. For further information call (800) ALABAMA.

Joseph Riley Smith Historic District—10th St. and 9th Ct. West. This area of black residential housing was built on the highlands of the original 1886 subdivision for prominent members of the Smith family as well as many of their corporate and professional colleagues. The district contains 64 houses and is a fine example of popular twentieth-century styles.

Kelly Ingram Park—5th Ave. North at 16th St. just northwest of the Sixteenth Street Baptist Church. The park played a pivotal role in Birmingham's civil rights movement and served as the meeting place for many major marches, demonstrations, rallies, and prayer services. A statue of Dr. Martin Luther King, Jr., stands in the park.

Nixon Building—1728 20th St. Built at the trolley crossing in 1922, this brick building's second floor dance hall was the center of black social life just prior to World War II. It was immortalized by big band composer Erskine Hawkins in "Tuxedo Junction."

Pilgrim Lutheran Church—447 1st St. North. (205) 251-3451. Reminiscent of a small, country black church, the Pilgrim Lutheran sits in the heart of Birmingham's Smithfield neighborhood. The 1930 structure is adorned with architectural elements symbolizing religious themes.

Ruth B. Jackson Cottage—1301 30th St. North. Mrs. Jackson, a leading black business woman, founded the Alabama Association of Modern Beauticians here in 1944. Her home now serves as its headquarters.

Sixth Avenue Baptist Church—1101 Martin Luther King, Jr., Dr. S.W. (205) 251-5173. The Sixth Avenue Baptist Church first opened its doors for worship on June 18, 1881. Not only does it now house one of the largest congregations in the state, but it has its own credit union for members. The church was rebuilt and moved to its present site in the early 1970s.

Sixteenth Street Baptist Church—1530 6th Ave., on the corner of 6th Ave. and 16th St. North. (205) 251-9402. Hours: by appointment only. Although the church was founded in 1873, the congregation's first sanctuary was not built until 1884. From its beginning, the church has served as a center for black community life. On September 15, 1963, during the racial unrest in the city, a fatal bomb explosion became a turning point in the civil rights protest in Birmingham and led to a rallying cry for unity throughout the country.

Smithfield Historic District—8th Ave. to 3rd St. West. The Smithfield community, located just a few blocks from Birmingham's Business District and the rich antebellum planter community of Elyton, was carved from the Joseph Riley Smith plantation. In November of 1886, Smith, along with nine other investors, incorporated the Smithfield Land Company. Six hundred acres of stubble field were subdivided as suburban lots. Streets were named for Smith's sons and grandsons, the avenues for their wives, daughters, and a few friends. By 1898, Smithfield was the fourth largest suburban community surrounding Birmingham with 297 households.

Trinity Baptist Church—328 4th Court North. (205) 252-9603. Massive and monumental for its site and neighborhood setting, this 1920 twin-tower church was constructed for Trinity Baptist Church and now houses the congregation of the New Mount Pilgrim Baptist Church. It is one of the two National Register churches in Alabama known to be the work of the Windham Brothers Construction Company.

Windham Construction Company Office Building—528 8th Ave. Formerly the home office for the family-owned and -operated business with branch offices in Nashville, Detroit, Indianapolis, and Chicago. The Windham Construction Company was noted for construction of significant public buildings as well as black residences in Smithfield.

BREWTON

Dooley Hall—North Rabb St. (Kirkland Rd.). Built in 1911, this two-story frame structure is the oldest building on the Southern Normal School campus, originally serving as the home of the school's founder, James Dooley, an African-American, and as a dormitory for its students. It is currently used for offices and classrooms.

CALHOUN

Hampton Cottage—Principal's Residence, Calhoun School, Lowndes County Rd. 33. Not open to the public. The two-story frame principal's residence is one of the three remaining structures from the historic period of Calhoun School, founded in 1892 as a vocational school for blacks on the advice of Booker T. Washington.

CARLTON

Hal's Lake—Off Clarke County Rd. 19. During the mid-1800s, Hal's Lake was named for a brave ex-slave who helped runaway slaves from surrounding states. The runaways hid on the shores of the lake before moving on to northern states.

Nebo Baptist Church and Cemetery (Effigy Cemetery)—Near Hal's Lake off Clarke County Rd. 19. Primarily for blacks, this cemetery is noted for its unique grave markers, many of which resemble the person buried beneath them.

CARROLTON

Pickens County Courthouse—Courthouse Square. (205) 367-8132. Hours: Mon.-Fri. 9-5. Visitors to the courthouse may spot the ghostly visage of Henry Wells, a black man convicted of robbery and other felonies during the 1800s. While Wells looked on in horror as a lynch mob gathered outside, a single bolt of lightning passed through the window, striking him dead and leaving his face permanently etched into the glass.

CENTREVILLE

Bibb County Training School—661 Montgomery Hwy. Site of the original 1889 school built by Henry Damon Davidson for blacks. The building burned, was rebuilt in the 1960s, then renamed the Davidson High School in his honor. Once the school was integrated, it became the Centerville Elementary School.

DAPHNE

Little Bethel Baptist Church—Main St. (205) 626-8182. On April 15, 1867, Major Lewis Starke deeded two acres of land to four ex-slaves and their heirs as trustees for the church which was to be built on this site. The adjoining cemetery marks the final resting place for Russell Dick, whose mother Lucy came to Mobile on the last voyage of the slave ship *Clotilde*. Dick is remembered as an outstanding and industrious citizen who acquired much land, once owning all of downtown Daphne.

DECATUR

Morgan County Courthouse—(Formerly Old Decatur Courthouse) at the corner of Ferry and Cain Sts. (205) 351-4600. In 1933, the Scottsboro Boys were retried here. The case led to the landmark Supreme Court decision that a defendant has the right to be judged by a panel of his peers, meaning black Americans could no longer be excluded from jury service.

DEMOPOLIS

Bluff Hall—407 N. Commissioners Ave. (205) 289-1666. Hours: Tues.-Sat. 10-4, Sun. 2-4. Built by slaves in 1832 when "cotton was king" on the white bluffs of the Tombigbee River, the plantation home was Allen Glover's wedding gift to his daughter. Corinthian columns grace the drawing room. A clothing museum and craft shop are included with period furnishings.

DOTHAN

Cherry Street African Methodist Episcopal Church— 308 North Cherry St. (205) 793-9664. In 1877, Gaines Chapel Church was organized and a wooden church was erected next to an existing graveyard. When the present Gothic structure was built in 1908, the name was changed. It is the mother church of the A.M.E. denomination in the state.

ELKMONT

Sulfur Trestle Fort Site—One mile south of Elkmont, seven miles north of Athens. During the Civil War, this 70-square-yard Union redoubt, manned by two companies of black troops (11th U.S. black troops, Col. Lathrop, commander) and the railroad trestle over Sulphur Creek were burned by Confederate General Nathan Bedford Forrest as part of his north Alabama raid to disrupt Union supply lines. The use of ex-slaves and free blacks was an experiment designed to free the regular troops for front-line duty.

FAIRFIELD

Miles College— 5500 Ave. G. (205) 923-2771. The colored Methodist Episcopal Church in Alabama established Miles College in 1898. The small co-educational institute continues to offer baccalaureate degrees in the traditional liberal arts disciplines.

FAIRHOPE

LeBanon Chapel A.M.E. Church—Young St. This church, listed on the National Register of Historic Places, is one of the most elaborately constructed buildings in Fairhope's historic black neighborhood.

Twin Beach A.M.E. Church—Twin Beach Rd. Organized in 1867 as Zion Chapel, the black congregation originally held services in a brush arbor. The present church was built in 1925.

FLORENCE

Peters Cemetery, Fieldstone Monument—Gunwaleford Rd. This monument, decorated with shells and figurines, makes reference to the 14th Amendment and honors slaves buried here.

St. Paul A.M.E. Zion Church—Cherokee St. Founded in 1860, the church was moved to its present site about 25 years ago. W.C. Handy's grandfather and father both served as pastors here. One of the church's highlights is the original stained glass window given by Handy's father.

W.C. Handy's Home and Museum—620 West College St. (205) 760-6434. Hours: Tues.-Sat. 9-noon and 1-4. Born in this log cabin in 1873, W.C. Handy is known as the "Father of the Blues." Restored to its original condition, the home has a small museum in the rear that contains memorabilia of W.C. Handy's life, including sheet music, photographs, souvenirs, his golden trumpet, and the piano on which he composed the "St. Louis Blues."

GADSDEN

Eleventh Street School—1026 Chestnut St. This school building remains largely unchanged since its construction in 1907. It is significant for its association with the growth of public education for blacks in the city.

GREENSBORO

St. Matthews A.M.E. Church. —1006 Morse St. in Hale County. Originally a Methodist church, St. Matthews is now part of the Greensboro Historic District, featuring nineteenth and twentieth century architectural styles common to the Black Belt regions of Alabama.

GREENVILLE

Butler Chapel A.M.E. Zion Church—407 Oglesby St. in Butler County. This imposing early twentieth century black-built design incorporates a variety of architectural elements suggesting both medieval and American colonial influences. The church has the earliest known black congregation in the city.

First Baptist Church—707 South St. This 1908 church sits atop a hill in the picturesque Baptist Hill community. It is one of only three black controlled institutions remaining in Greenville. Features include a steeply pitched roof line, an arched portico, and a grandiose belltower.

Ward Nicholson Corner Store—219 W. Parmer. This 1885 former general store stands as the earliest remaining evidence of black commerce in Greenville and one of the best examples of late 19th and early 20th century neighborhood black business districts.

GULF SHORES

Fort Morgan and Fort Gaines Historical Sites—Fort Morgan is located in Fort Morgan State Park, 21 miles west of Gulf Shores on AL 180. Fort Gaines is directly opposite, on East Bienville Blvd and AL 163. (205) 948-7275. Hours: Daily 9-5. Both forts guarded the Confederate seaport of Mobile and were significant Civil War battle sites that engaged black sailors. In August 1864, Admiral Farragut ("Damn the torpedoes, full speed ahead.") tried to pass the forts but came under heavy attack. John Lawson was one of the black men who served on the admiral's ship. Lawson, wounded by enemy gun fire, remained on the deck in the midst of battle until the forts were surrendered, and was later awarded the Congressional Medal of Honor for his bravery.

HAYNEVILLE

Lowndes County Courthouse—Washington St. (205) 548-2252. Built in 1856, then enlarged and modified in 1905, this two-story stucco and wood building is one of only four antebellum courthouses still in use in Alabama. During the civil rights movement, many significant trials were held here that led to fair hearings and representation of blacks on juries.

HOBSON CITY

Hobson City—"The City of Challenged Opportunity" was also Alabama's first black municipality. Originally a part of the city of Oxford, Hobson City in Calhoun County became a separate municipality in 1899 as boundaries were drawn to exclude the black settlement. More that 125 blacks were involved in creating the city of self determination where all men, women, and children are equal.

HUNTSVILLE

Oakwood College—Oakwood Rd. (205) 726-7000. A 4-year undergraduate, liberal arts institution founded in 1896 by the General Conference of the Seventh Day Adventists, Oakwood College was designed to provide educational opportunities for economically disadvantaged blacks.

St. Bartley Primitive Baptist Church—3020 Belafonte

Ave. N.W. (205) 536-6266. Organized by the Rev. William Harris during the late 1820s, this is one of the oldest black churches in the state. Services still held.

Watkins-Moore-Cummings-Rhett House—603 Adams St. Not open to the public. An elaborate spiral staircase dominates this antebellum home that was designed and built by former Virginia slave James Bell, who gained an unparalleled reputation for his stairways. This particular example took three years to build.

LEESBURG

Cedar Hill Methodist Church—Off U.S. Hwy 411 and State Rd. 68, (205) 526-8697. Founded in 1830 by a slave named Moses Hampton, Cedar Hill is considered the mother church of the Methodists. It was created when a band of travelers from the Carolinas stopped and asked permission from the Cherokee Indians to build a campsite. New settlers followed and built the church on the hill where Hampton prayed.

MARION

First Congregational Church of Marion—601 Clay St. The only Reconstruction period black church in Marion remaining without major modifications. It was built for and by the town's black congregation, many of whom were skilled in construction.

Gravesite of "Harry the Slave"—Marion Cemetery. Harry was the servant of Dr. Howard Talbird, president of Howard College, on the present site of Marion Institute. On October 15, 1854, he gave his life saving residents of the school from a fire.

Warreb (Georga) House—Lafayette St. Not open to the public. Slaves slept in underground rooms in this two-story frame dwelling, circa 1830.

MARTIN'S STATION

St. Luke's Episcopal Church—Dallas County Rd 21. This 1854 single-story church was one of the three antebellum board-and-batten Gothic Revival churches designed from plans by Richard Upjohn. During the 1930s, the church was given to the black St. Luke's congregation.

MILLER'S FERRY

Wilcox County Training School—Off State Rd. 28. (205) 682-4474. Established in 1884, Wilcox School is one of Alabama's oldest day schools. Judge William Henderson, a white Northerner who moved south after the Civil War, provided the land for the school in order for sharecroppers on his plantation to improve themselves. Henderson convinced the United Presbyterian Church of North America, of which he was a member, to provide the teachers.

MOBILE

Bettie Hunter Home—504 St. Francis St. Not open to the public. This black-built (1878) Italian-style home is comparable in scale, character and architectural detail to white-owned Mobile residences of the period. It was the home of Bettie Hunter (1852-1879), a former slave turned affluent Mobile businesswoman.

Dave Patton House—1252 Martin Luther King, Jr., Ave. Not open to the public. Dave Patton (1879-1927) was a successful black businessman who owned a hauling business in Mobile. He later expanded his business to include wrecking and contracting services. By 1910 he was noted as one of Mobile's most outstanding contractors employing 80 men and 40 mules.

Fine Arts Museum of the South—On Museum Dr. in

Langan Park. (205) 343-2667. Hours: Tues.-Sun. 10-5. This museum has a substantial collection of African art.

Magnolia Cemetery—Ann and Virginia Sts. in the southwest corner of Mobile. (205) 434-7307. This national cemetery contains the remains of Union soldiers who died during the 1865 capture of Mobile.

St. Louis Street Missionary Baptist Church—108 North Dearborn St. (205) 438-3823. One of the four black congregations established in Alabama prior to 1865, this is the second oldest Missionary Baptist Church in the city of Mobile. The present building, completed in 1872, hosted the 7th session of the Colored Baptist Convention in 1874, which established Selma University.

Slave Market Site—Corner of St. Louis and Royal Sts. Slaves were displayed and traded on this corner. It is also the site where the last cargo of slaves aboard the slaveship *Clotilde* came into the U.S. in 1859.

State Street A.M.E. Zion Church—502 State St. (205) 432-3965. Constructed in 1854, this antebellum church was one of the grandest built for a black congregation during this period. It is the oldest Methodist church in the city of Mobile, and one of only two black Methodist churches established in the city prior to the Civil War.

Stone Street Baptist Church—311 Tunstall St. (205) 433-3947. This structure was redesigned in 1931 at the height of the Depression by laymen who successfully utilized resources available to them. The black congregation's history dates back to the early nineteenth century.

U.S.S. *Alabama* **Battleship Park**—Located 1 1/2 miles east of Mobile on I-10, Battleship Parkway exit. (205) 432-5951. Hours: 8 a.m.-sunset. The U.S.S. *Alabama* participated in many Pacific World War II battles. The black W-Division served aboard the ship as cooks and stewards, and occasionally were called upon to handle gun powder during battles. Tours of the ship are available, along with tours of the submarine U.S.S. *Drum*, a B-52 bomber, and World War II fighter planes.

MONTGOMERY

Alabama Department of Archives and History—624 Washington Ave., State Capitol Complex. (205) 242-4363. Hours: Mon.-Fri. 8-5, Sat.-Sun 9-4:30. The nation's oldest state archives displays a unique collection of paintings honoring famous Alabamians and others whose achievements are connected with the state. Portraits of Martin Luther King, Jr., George Washington Carver, Booker T. Washington, Nat King Cole, W.C. Handy, Harper Trenholm and others are included. The building also houses the State History Museum and the genealogical research facilities.

Alabama State Capitol—1 Dexter Dr. Currently under reconstruction. Built in 1851, the Capitol building served the U.S. only ten years when, in 1861, it became the first Capitol of the Confederacy when Alabama seceded. The interior staircases are the work of Horace King, a noted black contractor and bridge builder. In 1965, after the march from Selma, civil rights marchers gathered on the Capitol steps which served as the scene for many other marches and demonstrations during the civil rights movement.

Alabama State University—915 South Jackson. (205) 293-4100. Founded in Marion, Alabama, in 1874 as a state normal school and university for colored students and teachers, Alabama State was relocated to Montgomery in 1887. The university's Levi Watkins Learning Arts Center has a special archives collection on the Montgomery bus boycott, Dr. E.D. Nixon's letters and papers, and related black history.

Ben Moore Hotel—Corner of Jackson and High Sts. No longer in operation. Built in the early 1950s, this hotel was prominent during the bus boycott of 1955-56. White city officials and black boycott leaders met in the roof garden restaurant.

Bethel Baptist Church—2106 Mill St. (205) 262-6825. Although the present church was built in 1977, Bethel's congregation dates back to 1867 and today has one of the largest black congregations in the city.

Beulah Baptist Church—3703 Rosa Parks Ave. (205) 265-2697. The church was incorporated in 1919, and like many area churches, has been used for services during the struggle for racial equality. The late singer Nat "King" Cole and his family attended church here when he was a boy. His father was one of the original members to assist with the church's incorporation; his mother played piano for the choir.

Carver Crafts Festival—An annual festival held each May that displays many African-American exhibits. For more information call (800) ALABAMA.

Centenniel Hill Historic District—Intersection and vicinity of Jackson and High Sts. Named Centennial Hill because its development began in 1876, this area remains a prominent black neighborhood today.

Church of the Good Shepherd—493 South Jackson St. (205) 834-9280. The only black Episcopal congregation in Montgomery. Built in 1900, the modest structure reflects a Gothic influence.

Civil Rights Memorial—Corner of Washington and Hull Sts. near the entrance to the Southern Poverty Law Center. Designed by Vietnam Memorial artist Maya Lin, the black marble memorial chronicles key events in the civil rights movement and is inscribed with the names of 40 people who lost their lives in the struggle for racial equality from 1955-68. The memorial was unveiled November 5, 1989.

Cole Samford House—1524 St. John St. Not open to the public. This simple one-story frame house was the birthplace and early childhood home of the jazz pianist and singer Nat "King" Cole (1919-1965).

Court Square—1 Court Square. Before the Civil War, Court Square served as a focal point in Montgomery for its slave, cotton and land auctions. In 1885, the city placed the fountain, topped by Hebe, the Goddess of Youth, over the artesian pool. In 1955, Rosa Parks boarded a Montgomery city bus directly across the street from the fountain and sat in a seat reserved for white patrons, starting a city wide bus boycott. During the Selma to Montgomery march in 1965, demonstrators passed this site on their way to the Capitol.

Dexter Avenue King Memorial Baptist Church—454 Dexter Ave. (205) 263-3970. Hours: Mon.-Fri. 8:30-noon, 1-4:30. Here Dr. Martin Luther King, Jr., continued his ministry and began his leadership as the driving force for civil rights. A mural in the basement of the church depicts major civil rights events and King's life. It is also an example of the role played by the black church in social reform.

Dr. E.D. Nixon Home—647 Clinton St. Not open to the public. Nationally recognized as a pioneer of civil rights, Dr. Nixon posted bail for segregation law violator Rosa Parks. In her defense, Dr. Nixon gathered the support of Montgomery blacks in implementing the successful 1955-56 Montgomery bus boycott. In spite of the bombing of this home and countless threats against his life, Nixon persistently fought racial segregation throughout the mid-twentieth century.

Dorsett-Phillips House—422 Union St. Not open to the public. This house was purchased in 1886 by Dr. Cornelius N. Dorsette, Montgomery's first black physician. He later became the chief of staff at Hale Infirmary.

First Baptist Church—347 North Ripley St. (205) 264-6921. Land for the church was purchased by ex-slaves in 1864; design was by Tuskegee architect W.T. Bailey. The present building replaced an earlier 1912 frame church. It is the birthplace of the Baptist State Convention U.S.A., Inc. (1880), and the first Institute of Nonviolence and Social Change sponsored by the Southern Christian Leadership Conference in 1957.

First Colored Presbyterian Church—310 North Hull St. in the Old Alabama Town Historic District. (205) 263-4355. Hours: Mon.-Sat. 9:30-3:30, Sun. 1:30-3:30. The small frame church dates from 1890 when black and white Presbyterians separated congregations. It has been restored to its original condition.

Holt Street Baptist Church—903 South Holt St. (205) 263-0522. On December 5, 1955, four days after Rosa Parks was arrested for riding in the front of a Montgomery city bus, the minister of Holt Street Baptist Church offered his church as a site of a mass meeting that would determine how long the community would abstain from riding city buses; more than 5,000 area blacks attended. The church was used many times for meetings and rallies during the civil rights movement.

Home of Nathan Alexander—503 Union St. Not open to the public. The noted Reconstruction Republican occupied this home until his death in 1915. He was also vice president of the Alabama Penny Savings Bank of Montgomery.

Jackson Community House—409 South Jackson St. This 1853 two-story clapboard house formerly served Montgomery's black community as a home for the elderly, an orphanage, a site for meetings and seminars, and, during one period, as the only library available to the black community until a public library became accessible.

McCall House—458 South Jackson St. Not open to the public. A significant example of Montgomery architecture, particularly the style used in the black Centennial Hill development.

Moore House—754 South Jackson St. Not open to the public. Built by Marshall J. Moore and his wife in 1900. Both were in the first graduating class of the State Normal School.

Montgomery Industrial School—515 Union St. Once the site of the Industrial School and the Booker T. Washington Elementary School, the school now serves as the Montgomery Teacher Center and offers classes in adult education through public schools.

Mt. Zion A.M.E. Zion Church—657 South Holt St. (205) 265-9361. A spectacular array of stained glass is the highlight of this church, which dates back to the 1890s.

North Lawrence-Monroe Street Historic District—Monroe and North Lawrence Sts. This area was noted as the major black business district which developed after the passage of Jim Crow Laws in the late nineteenth century. It is indicative of the black community's attempt to fulfill its social, cultural, and economic needs within the restrictive confines of racial segregation and discrimination.

Old Alabama Town Historic District—310 North Hull St. (205) 263-4355. Open Mon.-Sat. 9:30-3:30, Sun. 1:30-3:30. A walk through a restored neighborhood transports visitors to what life was like here a century ago. There are a number of carefully restored 1820s log cabins and an 1890s shotgun house (one room wide) that show contrast between early 1800s rural and urban homes.

Old Ship A.M.E. Zion Church—483 Holcombe St. (205) 262-3922. The Court Street Methodist Church built this church in 1834, then gave it to its black members in 1852, who moved it to its present site by rolling it on logs. Old Ship became the first black church in Montgomery.

Ordeman-Shaw Home—310 North Hull St., in the Old Alabama Historic District. (205) 263-4355. Hours: Mon.-Sat. 9:30-3:30, Sun. 1:30-3:30. This townhouse once employed city slaves who lived in the quarters above the kitchen. The restored home has simple furniture constructed by the slaves themselves.

Pastorium, Dexter Avenue Baptist Church—309 South Jackson St. Not open to the public. The home has served as the pastorium of the Dexter Avenue Baptist Church since 1919. This was home to Dr. Martin Luther King, Jr., during his ministry in Montgomery and his leadership of the Montgomery bus boycott.

Roots & Wings—1345 Carter Hill Rd. (205) 262-1700. Open Mon.-Sat. 10-6. Opened in November 1989, this magnificent structure houses an art gallery, theater, and bookstore. It showcases black paintings and graphic arts. Lectures, films and educational programs for children and adults are scheduled throughout the year. The works of nationally and internationally famous African-American writers are also displayed.

St. John A.M.E. Church—807 Madison Ave. (205) 265-

4136. The basement of this church, built in 1871, served as a school for area blacks until the 1880s.

St. John's Episcopal Church—113 Madison Ave. (205) 262-1937. Open Mon.-Fri. 8-5, Sat. 9-noon, Sun. 6a.m.-noon. After this Gothic-style church was constructed in 1855, the old St. John's (1837) was donated to the Negro Episcopalians, which meant the new St. John's was built without the usual slave gallery; the loft instead was designed for the organ and choir. Confederate President Jefferson Davis rented a pew in the church for his family; the pew and one of the old carpet-covered prayer stools remain in the church.

Southern Poverty Law Center—On the corner of Washington and Hull Sts. (205) 264-0286. The original building was destroyed by the Klan. As Klan killings and violence intensified in the 1970s, Morris S. Dees, co-founder and executive director of the center, began to represent the victims and their survivors. He also formed a unit of the center called Klanwatch, which monitors white supremacist groups. In 1981, Michael Donald, a black teenager, was lynched by the Klan. The center was responsible for bringing a law suit against the Klan that not only convicted one man for the murder, but also broke the entire Klan faction.

Swayne School Site—S.W. corner of Union and Grove Sts. In 1885, Swayne School was organized by the American Missionary Association and the Freedmen's Bureau following the Civil War.

Victor Tulane Home—430 Union St. Not open to the public. Victor Tulane came from Elmore County as a young black man in the late 1800s. He operated a grocery store at the corner of Ripley and High Streets for many years, worked for the American Penny Savings

Bank, Dean's Drug Store on Monroe Street, and later served on the Board of Trustees at Tuskegee Institute.

World Heritage Museum—119 West Jeff Davis Ave. (205) 263-7229. Hours: by appointment only. The museum includes photographs and a display on the history of the civil rights movement in Montgomery.

NORMAL

Alabama Agricultural and Mechanical University— Meridian St. (205) 851-5000. A bill was passed by the Alabama State Legislature in 1873 establishing Alabama A&M for the education of colored teachers. Today it offers bachelors, masters, and other professional programs.

OAKVILLE

Jesse Owens Monument—Off Alabama Hwy. 157, in southwest Lawrence County. The monument is dedicated to the memory of Olympic athlete Jesse Owens (1913-1980). In 1935-36 Owens broke three world records at college athletic meets. By winning the 100- and 200-meter dash, the 400-meter relay, and the broad jump at the 1936 Olympics in Berlin, Germany, he shattered Hitler's attempt to demonstrate Aryan superiority.

OPELIKA

Spring Villa—Springhill Rd. One of the best examples of early Gothic Revival architecture in Alabama, Spring Villa was constructed by William Penn Young as the focal point of his magnificently landscaped 455-acre plantation. Although Young probably served as his own architect, he may have been assisted by Horace King, a noted black builder of covered bridges and other structures. King, emancipated by Young's father-in-law in 1848, later became a state representative.

PHENIX CITY

John Godwin's Grave—Godwin's Cemetery in Russell County. This stunning monument was erected by Horace King, a former slave of bridge builder John Godwin. The marker was placed "In lasting remembrance of the love and gratitude he felt for his lost friend and former master."

Horace King Historical Marker—Corner of Dillingham and Broad Sts. Horace King, a slave of John Godwin, was a construction foreman for the first Dillingham Street Bridge in 1832, when he and Godwin introduced the Town Lattice bridge design to the Chattahoochee Valley. King built most of the early wooden bridges spanning the river, including those at West Point, Eufaula, and Fort Gaines Franklin. He was freed by an act of the Alabama Legislature in 1846 and later served in the Alabama House of Representatives.

PLATEAU, EAST MOBILE

Cudjoe Lewis Memorial—506 Bay Ridge Rd. in front of the Union Baptist Church. The *Clotilde*, the last slave ship to enter the United States reached Mobile in 1859. The ship's 130 slaves were freed at the start of the Civil War, and under the leadership of African Ka Zoola (Cudjoe Lewis), they created a village called Africa Town where they were able to retain their African customs, names, and language. The Africa Town settlement sprawls across Happy Hill, Plateau, and Magazine Point, and is the oldest African community in the state. Many of the *Clotilde* descendants still live in the area today.

Hopewell Baptist Church—Shelby St. (205) 456-9800.

The congregation was organized in 1898 and is still attended by many of the *Clotilde* descendants, the last slave ship into Mobile.

Mobile County Training School—800 Whitley St. (205) 456-7608. The first county training school established for blacks in the state. It is still in use today, providing training in the fields of agriculture, industry, and the arts.

Plateau Cemetery— Bay Ridge Rd. across from the Union Baptist Church. Final resting place of Cudjoe Lewis, one of the the last survivors of the slaveship *Clotilde*, along with many others who were aboard the ship and their descendants.

Yorktown Baptist Church—851 East Plateau St. The congregation was organized out of Union Baptist Church and is still attended by many descendants of the slaveship *Clotilde*.

PRICHARD

Africa Town, U.S.A. State Park—U.S.A. State Park, northeast of Mobile. Currently under construction, this will be the first park acknowledging African-American history in the country. Established by the Alabama State Legislature, the park will pay homage to the slaves aboard the ship *Clotilde*.

SELMA

Brown Chapel A.M.E. Church—410 Martin Luther King St. (205) 874-7897. Hours: by appointment only. Founded in 1867 as the first A.M.E. church in the state, the 1906 Byzantine-style chapel served as a headquarters for blacks during the civil rights movement. It was also the starting point for the march in 1965 from Selma to Montgomery, that was joined by Dr. Martin Luther King,

Jr. One room in the church is dedicated to Martin Luther King and contains memorabilia of that era. A monument of Dr. King sits in front of the church.

Concordia College—1804 Green St. (205) 874-5700. Formerly the Alabama Lutheran Academy and Junior College, the present Concordia College got its start when Miss Rosa Young approached the Lutheran Synodical Conference about her concern for spiritual and educational welfare of the area's black people. The two-year, co-educational college has been in operation since 1922.

Edmund Pettus Bridge—Hwy. 80, intersection of Broad St. and Water Ave. After departing from the Brown Chapel A.M.E. Church on the Selma to Montgomery march, civil rights marchers crossed this bridge that spans the Alabama River and were confronted by police. The violent conflict left 87 injured, outraged the nation and led to the passing of the Voting Rights Act of 1965.

First Baptist Church—Martin Luther King, Jr., St. Best known for the mass meetings and demonstrations held during the 1960s, which led to the passage of the Voting Rights Act. Built in 1894 and designed by a local black architect, it is considered one of the finer nineteenth-century black churches in the state.

Good Samaritan Hospital—Washington St. First founded by the Baptists in 1922, it was re-founded by the Fathers of St. Edmund, a Catholic religious order, in 1944. Victims of racial confrontation came here for treatment in 1965 during civil rights struggles. It was one of two predominantly black hospitals and today is a medical office building.

Historic Water Avenue—Water Ave. (205) 875-7241. A lovely nineteenth-century restored commercial district with brick streets, arcades and balconies overhanging the bluffs above the river. Three river-view parks offer historic sites within: Bienville Park, with historic marker and seating area; Songs of Selma Park, with a view of the famous Pettus Bridge, scene of a civil rights march; and Lafayette Park with historic buildings and picnic tables.

Martin Luther King, Jr., Street Church of God—Martin Luther King, Jr., St. A typical early black church (1900) built by the Sylvan Street Presbyterian Church, the second black Presbyterian congregation established in Alabama.

Old City Hall—Franklin St. Once served as both city and county jail in which Dr. Martin Luther King, Jr., and other civil rights protesters were imprisoned in 1965.

Old Depot Museum—Four Martin Luther King St., at the foot of Water Ave. (205) 875-9918. Hours: Mon.-Sat. 10-12 and 2-4, Sun.2-5. This museum features an array of exhibits that range from the Civil War to civil rights. Included are mementos of Dr. Martin Luther King, Jr., and the earlier black leader Benjamin Sterling Turner, an ex-slave who became Selma's first black congressman during Reconstruction.

Old Live Oak Cemetery—Hwy. 22, West Dallas Ave. Many slaves and prominent Selma residents are immortalized on tombstones and in statues including Benjamin Sterling Turner.

Rose Hill Cemetery—Beloit Rd. Burial ground for many ex-slaves.

Selma University—Lapsley and Jeff Davis Sts. (205) 872-2533. One of Alabama's early black colleges, Selma University was founded in 1866 by the Alabama Baptist Convention to train ministers and Christian teachers. The school now operates as a junior college.

Wilson Building—Franklin St. Erected in 1919 as the Dallas County Community Center, the building is decorated with striking murals of black life.

SNOW HILL

Snow Hill Institute—State Rds. 21 and 28. Site of the 1894 institute that once taught farming, carpentry, blacksmithing, painting, sewing, and housekeeping to area blacks.

TALLADEGA

Mt. Canaan Baptist Church—438 West Battle St. This church came into existence in 1870. Earlier members of Mt. Canaan were members of an early white church known as Good Hope Baptist Church. The name has been changed to the First Baptist Church of Talladega.

Talladega College—627 West Battle St. (205) 362-0206. This black liberal arts school was established by the American Missionary Association in 1867 as the first college open to all persons without regard to race in Alabama. Begun as a primary school, the college was incorporated in 1869. The college's Savery Library displays the Amistad Murals of the Cinque Mutiny, painted by black artist Hale Woodruff, which depict the historic 1839 event when slaves aboard a Spanish ship bound for Cuba, broke their chains and overtook the ship.

TUSCALOOSA

Beautiful Zion A.M.E. Church—Sanders Ferry Rd. (205) 759-2404. Organized in 1870 by freed blacks who had met for several years prior, it was originally established at Bush Arbor on Old Kenor and a church was built on the present site in 1896.

First African Baptist Church—2661 9th Ave. (205) 758-

2833. The oldest church bell in Tuscaloosa hangs in this church's belltower (1885). It is used today for weddings and special events.

President's Mansion—University Blvd. on the University of Alabama campus. (205) 348-6010. A notable example of Greek Revival architecture. The house was saved from destruction during the Civil War by the wife of the university president. The elaborate frescoes and medallions are all the work of slave labor.

Prewitt Slave Cemetery—Bull Slew Rd. Established by John Welsh Prewitt, veteran of the War of 1812. The cemetery was a burial ground for his slaves before and after the Civil War.

Stillman College—3600 15th St. (205) 349-4240. Founded in 1876 by the Presbyterian Church in the United States to train black ministers of the gospel. Today it is a four-year, fully accredited liberal arts college.

TUSCUMBIA

Alabama Music Hall of Fame—35674 Hwy. 72 West. (205) 381-4417. Hours: Mon.-Sat. 10-6, Sun. 1-6 p.m. Dedicated to honoring Alabama's "Music Achievers," the Alabama Music Hall of Fame holds memorabilia from the careers of Alabamians such as W.C. Handy and Nat King Cole. Exhibits include the step-by-step development of a record from songwriter to retail outlet and a recording facility that allows visitors to experience the magic of recording by singing to music tracks of their favorite songs.

TUSKEGEE

Booker T. Washington Monument—Tuskegee University. This statue on the Tuskegee University Campus depicts educator Booker T. Washington lifting the "Veil of Ignorance" from his fellow man.

Butler Chapel A.M.E. Zion Church—102 North Church St. Organized in the fall of 1865 by Rev. J.M. Butler, the chapel building was the first site of Tuskegee University.

Daniel "Chappie" James Center for Aerospace Science—Tuskegee University campus. (205) 727-8011. Hours: Mon.-Fri. 9-noon and 1-4, Sat.-Sun. by appointment. Daniel "Chappie" James was one of the university's better known students, becoming the country's first black four-star general. The aerospace center bearing his name was designed by Alabamian and Tuskegee graduate Tarlee W. Brown. The building houses the offices of the University's Army and Aerospace Sciences, Department of Aerospace Engineering, Health Education, and the memorial hall for General James.

George Washington Carver Museum—Tuskegee University campus. (205) 727-8011. Hours: Daily 9-5. This museum has a replica of Carver's early laboratory, his personal mementos, exhibits of the results of his research, and a biographical film on his life. The museum also contains an art gallery with examples of African art and sculpture.

Moton Field/Tuskegee Army Air Field—Tuskegee Municipal Airport off Chappie James Dr. (205) 727-8890. C. Alfred Anderson inspired the founding of the School of Aviation at Tuskegee University and became its chief instructor. He trained 966 blacks who became military aviators. Respectfully known as "Chief," Anderson turned out some of the best fighter pilots of World War II. The pilots in the original 99th Squadron performed so well they were joined by the 100th, 301st, and 302nd black fighter squadrons. Tuskegee, site of the annual

Fly-In, has been referred to as the "home of black aviation."

The Oaks—Tuskegee University campus. (205) 727-8011. Hours: daily 9-5. Booker T. Washington's home (c.1899) is now a museum operated by the National Parks Service. An excellent example of Victorian architecture, the home was designed by Robert Taylor, first black graduate of the Massachusetts Institute of Technology. It is one of the few surviving structures of this era designed and built by blacks.

Taska—On US 80, 5 1/2 miles east of Tuskegee. Follow the hiking trail along Choctafaula Creek for a beautiful walk through a tranquil pine grove. Look for a replica of an old log cabin where Booker T. Washington was born.

Tuskegee Institute National Historic Site—1212 Old Montgomery Rd. This historic site includes Booker T. Washington's home, the George Washington Carver Museum, and the Tuskegee University campus with more than 27 landmarks (built by students and faculty) associated with George Washington Carver and Booker T. Washington.

Tuskegee University—Old Montgomery Hwy. (205) 727-8011. The school was begun in 1881 when a bill, generated by Louis Adams, a former slave, and George W. Campbell, a slave owner, was passed by the Alabama State Legislature to establish a school for blacks in Macon County. Booker T. Washington became the school's first president. The campus Administration Building was originally the office of Booker T. Washington and is where the 12 feet x 26 feet Centennial Vision Mural is permanently displayed.

Tuskegee University Chapel—Tuskegee University

campus. Built in 1969 and designed by Paul Randolph. The original chapel (1896), designed by R.R. Taylor and built by university students, was destroyed by fire in 1957.

University Cemetery—Located near the Tuskegee Institute National Historic Site, 1212 Old Montgomery Rd. Both George Washington Carver and Booker T. Washington are buried here, along with other persons associated with the university.

Veteran's Administration Medical Center—North Tuskegee. (205) 727-0550. In 1921, this was the only hospital for black veterans of World War I. The center originally was comprised of 27 buildings.

WETUMPKA

Museum of Black History—1006 Lancaster St. (205) 567-5147. Hours: by appointment only. This was the first county training school for blacks in Elmore County (1925). The training school served the county and trained students in many areas. The museum contains past and present memorabilia of the county's black residents.

WHISTLER/PRICHARD

Whistler Historic District—Bounded by Eight Mile Creek, US 45, I-65 and the Prichard corporate limits in Mobile County. Dating from before the Civil War, the black community of Whistler is in the oldest part of the Prichard area. The district contains home and transportation landmarks from Whistler's early days as an industrial center for building railroad boxcars.

WHITEHALL

Holy Ground Battle Park—Off Hwy. 80 in Lowndes County. Hours: 9a.m.-8p.m. This outstanding recreational facility located in the Black Belt is currently the largest park in Alabama in a predominantly black community. The park has a public playground, picnicking, beach area, swimming, fishing, and hiking trails.

LOUISIANA

The Louisiana landscape of steamy cypress swamps, dense pine forests and mazelike bayous, has played host for centuries to an eclectic blend of cultures and races. Its name alone evokes a mosaiclike image of diverse faces, spirited music, and raucous good times.

Named for King Louis XIV, the region we now call Louisiana was claimed by French settlers in 1682. Precisely when Africans were first brought to the area is unknown, but in 1712 the colony claimed to have twenty black slaves. By 1719, a much larger number had arrived, and in 1724 the Code Noir (Black Code), a system of laws regulating slavery, was first enacted. During its time, the Code Noir was considered a rather lenient and generous system when compared to those in other slave colonies. Under French rule, black slaves were granted a certain number of rights and privileges. They were even allowed to give their own masquerade balls and festivals, and Congo Square in New Orleans was created just for this purpose. After France seceded Louisiana to Spain in 1762, Spanish settlers began to bring larger numbers of slaves to Louisiana. In the 1790s many whites and free blacks from the nearby West Indies settled in the area, and the Spanish civil code expanded the rights of blacks. In 1800 Spain ceded Louisiana back to France and in 1803 it was purchased by the United

States. By the time Louisiana became a state in 1812, nearly all of the rights of blacks were eliminated under the American slave system.

During its early history, an important characteristic of the Louisiana culture was the development of the so-called Creole population. Originally, the term *Creole* referred to native-born people of French or Spanish ancestry. During slavery it was used to describe native-born French-speaking slaves, as opposed to imported slaves from Africa or English speaking areas. With time, *Creole* came to mean all native-born Louisianans (excluding native Indians) whether they were white, black, or of mixed race. The black Creoles of Louisiana today are mixed descendants of Europeans, Africans, and West Indians.

Interracial marriage was not uncommon. The resulting population, which became quite substantial, has through the years been subject to both privileged status and drastic discrimination. Blacks and mulattoes, during the state's early history, were laced throughout all levels of Louisiana society—from slaves to plantation owners, servants and businessmen. But after the Louisiana Purchase the Creoles lost much of their power to English-speaking Americans.

From the early to mid-1800s, Louisiana developed a plantation economy based on cotton, rice, corn, sugar and indigo that was dependent on slave labor.

Also at this time the practice of voodoo became common place in the state. A religion that combined West African traditions brought by slaves and the practices of the Catholic Church followed by European settlers, voodoo became an everyday fact of life that was practiced by both slaves and upper class Creoles. Marie Laveau, the acclaimed Creole voodoo queen of New Orleans, developed a devoted following. Today, voodoo remains a part of Louisiana life and the New Orleans Historic Voodoo Museum pays tribute to the great voodoo queen.

In 1861, Louisiana joined the Southern states in seceding from the Union. Following the Civil War, the state enforced restrictive racial codes and a period of civil unrest began. In 1866 a brutal race riot erupted in New Orleans when a parade of blacks marched through the streets protesting the injustices of the state constitution. When it ended, 34 blacks were dead. In 1868 a new state constitution granted suffrage to blacks and Louisiana was readmitted to the Union.

The 1870s brought more strife. Although a few achievements of blacks can be noted—Oscar Dunn served as lieutenant governor, and Pickney Benton Stuart Pinchback briefly served as acting governor and started the *Louisianan* newspaper that took up the defense of blacks—for the most part white hostilities escalated and their opinions were voiced through the Ku Klux Klan and the Knights of White Camellia. In 1898, the government imposed a new constitution that withheld the right to vote from blacks by means of literacy tests. Whites were excluded from the tests under a convoluted "grandfather clause."

At about this time, when the oppression of blacks in the state once again became severe, one of America's most original art forms, the music known as jazz, was born. Conceived in New Orleans and originally called "jass," the music grew out of the traditional black sounds of ragtime and blues. In the early 1900s countless brass bands performed throughout the city in open-air parks. Soon after, the music spread across the South and then the country. Many great jazz legends were born in Louisiana including Louis Armstrong, Joe "King" Oliver and Jelly Roll Mortin.

During the civil rights era of the 1960s, Louisiana underwent drastic social changes that were accompanied by periods of forceful resistance by segments of the white population; several school desegregation plans required federal interventions. Although today the state has reached a level of cultural harmony that includes great pride among the many ethnic groups of the state, the black population which represents about 30 percent, must still grapple with racial divides. A recent example of white backlash was apparent in the unsuccessful bid for the governorship by former Ku Klux Klan leader David Duke.

LOUISIANA SITES

For general travel information contact the Louisiana Department of Tourism: P.O. Box 94291, Baton Rouge, LA 70804-9291. (504) 342-8119, or toll-free outside Louisiana (800) 334-8626. For information on black tourism, contact the Greater New Orleans Black Tourism Network, 1530 Sugar Bowl Dr., New Orleans, LA 70112. (504) 523-5652, or toll-free outside Louisiana (800) 725-5652.

BATON ROUGE

Port Hudson State Commemorative Area and Museum—756 W. Plains-Port Hudson Rd., Zachary, 14 miles north of Baton Rouge on US 61. (504) 654-3775. Hours: Wed.-Sun. 9-5. A 650-acre park that encompasses part of the Port Hudson Battlefield, a Civil War site that witnessed the longest siege in U.S. military history. Several times in the summer of 1863, Confederate-held Port

Booker T. Washington lifts the "Veil of Ignorance" at Tuskegee University. (Alabama Department of Tourism)

Log cabin where W.C. Handy was born in Florence, AL. (Alabama Department of Tourism)

Carver Museum is at Tuskegee. (Alabama Department of Tourism)

Black granite table and wall are focal points of civil rights memorial in Montgomery. (Alabama Department of Tourism)

Edmund Pettus Bridge, site of Bloody Sunday in 1965, crosses the Alabama River in Selma. (Alabama Department of Tourism)

Benjamin Sterling Turner (1825-1894) was Selma's first congressman. (Alabama Department of Tourism)

The formal ceremony transferring the Louisiana Territory to the United States took place on the second floor of the Cabildo in New Orleans French Quarter. (Louisiana Department of Tourism)

The exterior of the Cabildo on Jackson Square shows a variety of architectural forms. (Louisiana Department of Tourism)

The Rural Life Museum in Baton Rouge is part of the Burden Plantation. (Louisiana Department of Tourism)

On the front porch of this house in Henning, Tennessee, young Alex Haley heard stories which later became the basis for **Roots.** *(Tennessee Department of Tourism)*

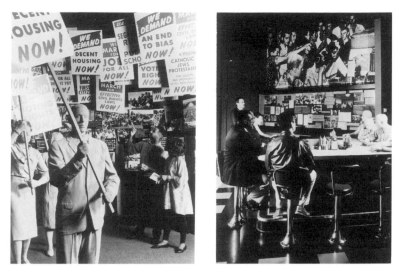

The Civil Rights Museum in Memphis brings the sights, sounds and exhilaration of the early 60s to life. (Tennessee Department of Tourism)

Mud Island in Memphis showcases the history, folklore and culture of the Mighty Mississippi. (Tennessee Department of Tourism)

The terminal for the Chattanooga Choo Choo is now a complex of shops, retaurants and gardens. (Tennessee Department of Tourism)

Beale Street in Memphis was "the birthplace of the blues." (Tennessee Department of Tourism)

Dunleith is a Greek Revival mansion in Natchez where John R. Lynch served as a house servant before he became an influential political voice. (Mississippi Department of Tourism)

Longwood is just one of many striking mansions in the Natchez area. (Vera Stevens)

Canary Cottage was the home of Charlotte Hawkins Brown.
(North Carolina Department of Tourism)

Dr. Charlotte Hawkins
Brown. (North Carolina
Department of Tourism)

Charlotte Hawkins Brown Memorial remembers the educator.
(North Carolina Department of Tourism)

Rag man is member of
Durham American Dance
Ensemble at homecoming
event at Somerset Place.
(North Carolina Department
of Tourism)

Somerset Place offers visitors a glimpse of 19th century planta-tion life. (North Carolina Department of Tourism)

The Mary McLeod Bethune Statue is located in Lincoln Park, NE. (Washington, D.C. Department of Tourism)

Cedar Hill in Anacostia was the last residence of Frederick Douglass. (Washington, D.C. Department of Tourism)

Visitors to Colonial Williamsburg are encouraged to participate in the Black Music program. (Virginia Department of Tourism)

Reconstructed slave cabin in Rocky Mount commemorates Booker T. Washington. (Virginia Department of Tourism)

Interpreters portray slaves in the kitchen at Wetherburn Tavern in Colonial Williamsburg. (Virginia Department of Tourism)

Hudson was attacked by the 1st and 3rd Louisiana Regiments which consisted of 1,000 free blacks from New Orleans. Forced to retreat from the mortar blasts of the well-defended garrison, the black troops suffered severe bloodshed and lost 212 men. The grounds today consist of trails along the battlefield trenches, outdoor exhibits, guided tours and a museum that explains the historic event.

Southern University—North of Airline Hwy., just off Scenic Hwy. (504) 771-2430. Founded in 1880, Southern University is one of the largest predominately black universities in the U.S. Attractions include the student union and its gallery, the "Red Stick" monument, the quarters of the Southern Jaguar mascot—LaCumb—and the Black Heritage Exhibit Series at the university's library. Guided tours of the campus are available with advance reservations.

Tabby's Blues Box Heritage Hall—1314 North Blvd. (504) 387-9715. Hours: Mon., Wed., Thurs. 3p.m.-11p.m.; Fri.-Sat 3p.m.-2a.m.; Sun. 5p.m.-11p.m. A must for blues fans, Tabby's features live music most nights of the week including blues favorites Silas Hogan, Guitar Kelly and Tabby Thomas.

DERRY

Magnolia Plantation—LA 119, one mile north of Derry and 40 miles north of Alexandria. (318) 379-2221. Hours: daily 1-4. A Creole-style plantation house built in 1784 that was destroyed during the Civil War and rebuilt to its original condition. In addition to the 27-room house, there are several outbuildings, barns, a chapel, blacksmith shop, cotton press, and a row of tiny, brick slave houses.

HOMER

Ford Museum—519 Main St. (318) 927-3271. Hours: Mon.-Fri. 10a.m.-noon, 1:30-4; Sat. 10-2; Sun.2-4. An exhibit that explores the blend of Scotch-Irish and African-American cultures that makes up the area's heritage.

KENNER

Kenner—A Mississippi River town west of New Orleans that throughout history has had a predominately black population, many members of which have made significant contributions to the area. In addition to the town's historic Rivertown District and historical museum, points of interest include the Louisiana Toy Train Museum, Wildlife and Fisheries Aquarium, and the Saints Hall of Fame.

Kenner Historical Museum—1922 Third St., on LA 48. (504) 469-6196. Hours: Sat. 10-noon, or by appointment. The museum houses memorabilia and artifacts dating back to the 1700s from Kenner and Jefferson Parish with a special showroom on black history.

MANSFIELD

Mansfield State Commemorative Area—On LA 175 four miles southeast of Mansfield. (318) 872-1474. Hours: Wed.-Sun. 8-4:30. Site of the last major Confederate victory of the Civil War, it was at the Mansfield battlefield that an advance by Union General Nathaniel P. Banks and his troops, including four regiments of black infantry, was brutally halted in 1864. The area includes self-guided walking tours of the battlefield and an historical museum with slide presentations and relics from the Civil War.

MELROSE

Melrose Plantation—Two miles east of LA 1 on LA 493 (119), 15 miles south of Natchitoches. (318) 379-0055. Hours: daily noon-4. Marie-Therese Coincoin, a freed slave, founded a unique Franco-African community in 1796 around what is now Melrose Plantation. The community of Creole blacks, many of whom owned their own slaves, grew to a substantial number in the 1800s. Coincoin's original home named Yucca, still stands as does the 1800 African House, the only colonial era, African-style structure standing in the U.S. today. Following an introductory film, the tour of the grounds includes Yucca House, Africa House, the big house which is still furnished with period antiques, and painter Clementine Hunter's 1950s murals.

NEW ORLEANS

A.L. Davis Park—Corner of LaSalle St. and Washington Ave. Formerly Shakespeare Park, it was dedicated in honor of the late Rev. A.L. Davis. The park was the site of many civil rights rallies prior to the late 1960s. On September 10, 1963, the Citizens Committee of New Orleans marched from this park to City Hall with a petition of civil rights grievances.

Amistad Research Center—6823 St. Charles St. in Tulane University's Tilton Hall. (504) 865-5535. Hours: daily 8:30-5. Founded in 1966 by the American Missionary Association, the Amistad Center houses the largest American ethnic historical archives in the world. It contains over a million manuscripts dating from the late 1700s to the present with more than 90 percent of these on black-white relations, and a display of African and African-American art.

Armstrong Park—North Rampart and St. Ann Sts. This

park was dedicated on April 15, 1980, in memory of the great jazz musician Louis "Satchmo" Armstrong. The park's statue of Armstrong was sculpted by Elizabeth Catlett, a noted black artist. A unique urban garden, Armstrong Park is where many festivals and concerts are held. Inside the park in front of the municipal auditorium is Congo Square, the spot where slaves met for traditional African song and dance during colonial and antebellum times.

Bourbon Street Gospel and Blues Club—227 Bourbon St. (504) 523-3800. Hours: 11a.m.-1a.m. An outdoor club that specializes in gospel and blues performances and a down-home weekend gospel brunch.

Cabildo—Corner of Chartres and St. Peter Sts. (504) 568-6968. Hours: Wed.-Sun. 9-4. A government office building built in 1795, the Cabildo is a combination of Spanish and French architecture. It is where the historic Louisiana Purchase took place, and is now owned by the Louisiana State Museum and houses many artifacts by and about African-Americans.

Chalmette National Historical Park—Six miles downriver from the French Quarter on LA 46, (504) 589-4428. Hours: daily 8:30-5. The last battle of the War of 1812 was fought on this site on January 8, 1815, when the English tried to capture New Orleans. But the British troops couldn't conquer the Americans who included Creoles, Indians, and free blacks. One of the heroes of the battle was a young black drummer whose drumbeat kept the troops together during the thick fog. The park's visitor center includes an audio-visual center and exhibits on the battle. Self-guided auto tours are available.

Chez Helene Restaurant—316 Chartres St. (504) 525-6130. Hours: Sun.-Thurs. 7a.m.-10p.m., Fri.-Sat. 7a.m.-

11p.m. A casual restaurant that offers some of the best Creole soul food in the South.

Convent of the Sisters of the Holy Family—6901 Chef Menteur Hwy. (504) 523-2222. Founded in 1842 in New Orleans by Harriette Delille, this is the second order of black nuns founded in the U.S. The convent's original location at 717 Orleans Ave. in the French Quarter once housed an orphanage, convent and school; it is now the Bourbon Orleans Hotel.

Davis Gallery—904 Louisiana Ave. (504) 897-0780 or 895-5206. Hours: Mon.-Sat 10-5, and by appointment. African tribal art including authentic masks, figures, costuming, jewelry, weapons and ethnographia from West Africa.

Dew Drop Inn Cafe and Bar—2836 La Salle St. Now an empty building, the Dew Drop Inn was the most famous African-American nightclub in New Orleans during the 1940s and 50s. In its early years, whites were forbidden to enter due to strict segregation laws. But eventually, it opened its doors to everyone and hosted such great performers as Dinah Washington, Little Richard, Ray Charles, and Ella Fitzgerald.

Dillard University—2601 Gentilly Blvd. (504) 283-8822. A private, co-educational, undergraduate liberal arts college with historical roots dating back to 1869. Named for James Dillard who aided the advancement of black education in the 1800s, Dillard University formulated a pre-freshmen study program which became the model for the national Upward Bound program. The campus has impressive architecture and beautiful gardens, and the Alexander Library holds an extensive collection of material on African-American history and music.

Dooky Chase—2301 Orleans Ave. (504) 821-0600. Hours:

Sun.-Thurs. 11:30 a.m.- midnight, Fri.-Sat. 11:30a.m.-1a.m.; reservations suggested. One of the finest restaurants in New Orleans, Dooky Chase is not only a favorite among blacks, but it also has a cult-like international following. In addition to serving some of the best fried chicken, Creole jambalaya, sweet potatoes and greens, Dooky Chase is as much noted for its collection of black American folk art as it is its food.

Dryades St. YMCA School of Commerce—2222 Ortheas Castle Haley Blvd. (504) 522-8811. In one of the oldest business districts in New Orleans, the Dryades YMCA was founded in 1905 as the "Colored Young Men's Christian Association." It offer educational, recreational, vocational and technical training programs for area youths.

Fats Domino's Home—Caffin Ave. and Marais St. Not open to the public. This working-class neighborhood house is where Antoine Domino grew up.

French Market—800-100 Decatur St. Hours: Open 24-hours a day with a flea market on weekends. An historic collection of several buildings containing many stalls where black and white vendors sell foods and crafts.

Hermann-Grima Historic House—820 Saint Louis St. (504) 525-5661. Hours: Mon.-Sat 10-3:30. One of the earliest and best examples of American architecture in the French Quarter, this restored 1821 mansion once served as home to a wealthy Creole family. The house is surrounded by a stable, courtyards, and slave quarters. Tours of the mansion include an interpretation of the family's lifestyle and Creole cooking lessons.

Jackson Square—801 Decatur St. in the French Quarter. Since its origins in 1720, Jackson Square has been the site of many historic events including the transfer ceremonies of the Louisiana Purchase; it is one of the most most popular city squares in the country. Named for General Andrew Jackson who was welcomed here after the victory of his black and white troops in the Battle of Chalmette during the War of 1812. Beautiful buildings with wrought and cast ironwork, many constructed by black craftsmen, surround the square.

Jane Alley—Between Loyola and S. Rampart Sts. across from City Hall. This one-block street, now part of a parking lot, was were Louis Armstrong was born in 1900. Only a tree remains where his house once stood. In the early 1900s, Jane Alley was a rough-neck neighborhood full of hustlers, pimps, and thieves.

Joseph Bartholomew Memorial Park Golf Course— 6514 Congress Dr. (504) 288-0928. Hours: Mon.-Sun. 6a.m.-5:30 p.m. A public golf course named in honor of Joseph Bartholomew, a black golf course architect who designed and built several golf courses in the New Orleans area.

Knights of St. Peter Claver—1825 Orleans Ave. (504) 821-4225. The Knights of St. Peter Claver is a predominately black fraternal order. Its current structure serves as the national headquarters of the organization.

La Belle Gallery—309 Chartres St. (504) 529-3080. Hours: daily 10-7. A fine art gallery specializing in African-American sculptures, paintings, ceramics, prints, posters, and a collection of African antiques.

Lulu White's Mahogany Hall—309 Bourbon St. (504) 525-5595. Hours: daily 12p.m.-12:45a.m. One of the first jazz clubs on Bourbon Street, Lulu White's is named for one of city's most famous madams. It offers first-rate Dixieland jazz amid turn-of-the-century ambience.

Martin Luther King, Jr., Statue—Martin Luther King

Blvd. and South Clairborne Ave. A statue dedicated to Dr. King by the citizens of New Orleans on January, 15, 1981. Annual ceremonies are held here in honor of his birthday.

Musee Conti Museum of Wax—917 Conti St. (504) 525-2605. Hours: daily 10-5:30. The wax museum of Louisiana legends, Musee Conti is world-famous for its costumed, life-size figures depicting New Orleans history from 1699 to the 1900s. Wax sculptures include voodoo queen Marie Laveau and her voodoo dancers, Louis Armstrong, a slave auction, and the home of Madame Lalaurie, a vicious woman who mistreated her slaves so severely that she was forced to leave New Orleans.

New Orleans Historic Voodoo Museum—724 Dumain St. (504) 523-7685. Hours: Sun.-Thurs. 10-dusk, Fri.-Sat. 10a.m.-10p.m. A fascinating museum featuring an account of New Orleans voodoo and Louisiana hoodoo. Occult-related displays include voodoo dolls, instruments for ritual music, African masks and carvings, and a history of voodoo queen Marie Laveau. The museum also offers voodoo tours of the French Quarter and nearby bayous and Indian burial grounds.

New Orleans Jazz and Heritage Festival Offices—1205 North Rampart St. (504) 522-4786. Hours: Mon.-Fri. 9-5. The New Orleans Jazz and Heritage Foundation, a non-profit organization dedicated to the promotion and preservation of the cultural heritage of Louisiana, sponsors the New Orleans Jazz Heritage Festival and other musical events.

New Orleans Jazz Club Collection and Jazz Museum—400 Esplanade in the Old U.S. Mint. (504) 522-4786. Hours: Tues.-Sun. 10-6. A permanent exhibit on the history of jazz in New Orleans including documents, photographs, videos, rare recordings, Louis Armstrong's first trumpet, and a Mardi Gras exhibit.

New Orleans Museum of Art—Lelong Ave. in City Park. (504) 488-2631. Hours: Tues.-Sun. 10-5. The museum's permanent collection includes paintings, sculptures and decorative arts from Africa.

New Zion Baptist Church—2319 Third St. (504) 891-4283. New Zion is the site where the Southern Christian Leadership Conference was formed in 1956. During that time, the late Rev. A.L. Davis, the first black councilman of New Orleans, marched from this church to City Hall with a petition of grievances. Services are still held.

Ursulines Convent—1114 Chartres St. The Sisters of St. Ursula, who came to New Orleans from France in 1727, moved into this structure in 1749. The first nunnery in Louisiana, Ursulines Convent operated the first Indian school, black school, and orphanage in the state. The sisters have moved to a new location in the city and the Archdiocese of New Orleans is presently restoring this historic building.

Pete Fountain's—2 Poydras St. in the New Orleans Hilton. (504) 523-4374. Hours: Tues., Wed., Fri., Sat. 9p.m.-11:15p.m. A 500-seat club that offers New Orleans jazz by the legendary clarinetist.

Pontalba Buildings—523 St. Ann St. on Jackson Square. Completed in 1851 by Barones Micaela Pontalba, the Pontalba buildings are some of the oldest apartment buildings in the U.S. Many years ago, the buildings housed the law office of noted black attorney and notary public Rene C. Metoyer.

Preservation Hall—726 St. Peter St. (504) 522-2841. Hours: daily 8:30p.m.-12:30a.m. The oldest Masonic temple in Louisiana dating back to 1820, Preservation Hall is considered one of the bastions of traditional New Orleans jazz. In its early years it was a meeting place for "free men and women of color," and later went on to become a center for jazz bands and dances. Preservation Hall still hosts nightly concerts by jazz veterans and newcomers to the field.

St. Louis Cathedral—700 Chartres St. (504) 525-9585. One of the oldest churches in the country, St. Louis was supported by black philanthropists Marie Leveau and Thomy Lafon.

St. Louis Cemetery Number 1—425 Basin St. (504) 596-3050. Hours: daily 9-3. An historic city cemetery where many noted blacks are buried including Pickney Benton Stewart Pinchback, the first black lieutenant governor during Reconstruction; and the famed voodoo queen Marie Laveau who cured the sick and the lovelorn with her magic spells during the 1800s. Although a few historians say that Laveau was buried in nearby St. Louis Cemetery Number 2, most believe that her body in fact lies in the Number 1 tomb marked simply with the name Laveau. Nearby St. Louis Cemeteries Number 2 and Number 3 also contain the remains of many notable New Orleans blacks.

Snug Harbor—626 Frenchman St. (504) 949-0696. Hours: Nightly 6p.m.-2a.m. One of the city's best choices for modern jazz and full-course meals.

Southern University at New Orleans—6400 Press Dr. (504) 286-5000. The largest predominately black university in New Orleans, Southern University is a liberal arts college led by the first black woman chancellor in the area, Dr. Dolores Spikes.

Specialty Tours —421 Manasses Pl. (504) 282-1932 (Telephone lines open 24 hours a day). A tour operator specializing in unique themes such as walking tours in jazz areas, black heritage, and voodoo.

Tripitina's—501 Napolean Ave. (504) 895-8477. Hours: Mon.-Fri. 11a.m.(?), Sat.-Sun. 2p.m.(?). Called New Orleans's best nightclub, Tripitina's offers a variety of jazz, R&B, and Cajun music in a large, two-level setting.

U.S. Custom House—423 Canal St. (504) 589-6353. Hours: Mon.-Fri 9-5. Built in 1849, this government building once served as headquarters for a large fraction of black Republicans. It later became an important place of employment for many blacks including Walter L. Cohen, Comptroller of Customs, and A.P. Turead, noted civil rights attorney.

Xavier University—7325 Palmetto St. (504) 486-7411. Founded in 1915, Xavier University is the only predominately black Roman Catholic university in the Western Hemisphere. The university is noted for being the second largest of the 41-member colleges of the United Negro College Fund, and for being among the top five universities in the U.S. in placing black graduates in medical school.

ST. FRANCISVILLE

Cottage Plantation—On US 61 about 50 miles south of Natchez, (504) 635-3674. Hours: daily 9-5. One of the oldest and largest remaining sugar plantations in Louisiana, Cottage Plantation's beautiful antebellum buildings were built by slave labor. Restored structures on the grounds include a schoolhouse, smokehouse, kitchen, milkhouse, carriage house, and slave quarters.

VACHERIE

Oak Alley Plantation—3645 LA Rt. 18, midway between

Baton Rouge and New Orleans. (504) 265-2151. Hours: daily 9-5. Slave labor was primarily responsible for the construction of this Greek Revival mansion that is considered to be one of the best known in the Old South.

TENNESSEE

Although Tennessee is located between the Deep South and the Midwest, it is a state of the upper South in its traditions. Despite an economy based on small towns and small farms, Tennessee was a slave state, with slaves comprising 26 percent of the population in 1860. Most of its people enthusiastically supported the Confederacy, and Tennessee was a major western Civil War battleground.

Fort Pillow in Henning was the site of a particularly bloody battle. Taken originally by Union Forces in 1862, it was recaptured by Confederate troops in 1864. The few black survivors of the battle later testified before the Federal Committee on the Conduct of the War that following the Union surrender Confederate troops massacred many survivors.

Henning is notable also as the birthplace of the late Alex Haley, whose book "Roots" inspired a generation of African-Americans to search for their own.

Nashville, located in the north central part of the state, is distinguished by several black institutions of higher learning, including Meharry Medical School, one of the leading training centers for black doctors in the United States. Fisk University, founded as Fisk Free School in 1866 by the Freedman's Bureau, owes much of its current renown, if not its very existence, to the Fisk Jubilee

Singers, a school chorus founded in 1871. At that time, the school was in serious trouble, with no heat and no food for its students. The chorus was formed to raise funds for the school by giving concerts.

Not only did the Fisk Jubilee Singers make the school solvent, but once they began including spirituals in their repertoire, they created a new appreciation for the so-called "slave songs" that had formerly represented in the minds of blacks a time that was best forgotten. Through their tours, including two European tours in the 1870's, the Fisk Jubilee Singers created a world audience for the Negro spiritual.

In more recent times, Fisk University was the site of early student sit-ins in support of the first sit-ins by students at North Carolina Agricultural and Technical College. Marion Barry, later mayor of Washington, D.C., and Diane Nash, who would become an activist in the Student Nonviolent Coordinating Committee, were among the Fisk students who spearheaded the effort in Nashville.

While Nashville became the capital of country music, Memphis, located on the Mississippi River in the western part of the state, cradled the blues. Although born in Alabama, W.C. Handy composed his first blues songs in Memphis. A statue of Handy now overlooks W.C. Handy Park on Beale Street.

Memphis was also the site of a sad, more recent event in African-American history, for it was there at the Lorraine Motel that Dr. Martin Luther King, Jr. was assassinated on April 4, 1968.

TENNESSEE SITES

For general travel information contact the Tennessee

Department of Tourism, P.O.B. 23170, Nashville, TN 37202 or call (615) 741-2158.

CHATTANOOGA

African Cultural Ball —(615) 267-1076. An annual event that begins February 1st and kicks off the Chattanooga African-American Museum's celebration of Black History Month.

Booker T. Washington State Park —State Highway 58/Rt.2. (615) 894-4955. Hours: Daily 8-sunset. The shores of the Chattanooga Lake provide a perfect setting for fishing and boating enthusiasts. The park also offers a swimming pool and a group camp.

Chattanooga Afro-American Museum and Research Center—730 Martin Luther King Blvd., (615) 267-1076. Hours: Mon.-Fri. 9-5. Dedicated to the study of black culture and intellectual values, the museum has exhibits on the black history of Chattanooga, African-American and African arts, photographs, historical documents and library. A special collection is devoted to Tennessee native Bessie Smith. Known as the "Queen of Blues," Smith belted out the blues across the country until her tragic death in 1937. Included in the exhibit are Smith's upright piano, recordings, and personal memorabilia.

HENNING

Alex Haley Home and Museum— 200 S. Church St. and Haley Avenue. Henning is 45 miles north of Memphis on TN 209. (901) 738-2240. Hours: Tues.-Sat. 10-5, Sun. 1-5. A state-owned historic site, the Alex Haley Home and Museum marks the boyhood home of Alex Haley, the Pulitzer Prize-winning author of "Roots." It pays tribute to the Haley family through displays of family portraits, mementos and furnishings from the period, and is an excellent example of rural Tennessee life of the early 1900's. A tour of the home includes lessons on lye soap-making and sausage grinding, and a glimpse of the original piano used to entertain the family over 60 years ago. The grave of Chicken George, the author's famous ancestor, can be viewed in the nearby Bethlehem Cemetery.

Bethlehem Cemetery—Durhamville Road, one mile east of Henning. The cemetery's second entrance leads directly to the Haley family plot and the grave of Chicken George.

Fort Pillow State Historic Area—On TN 87 approximately 18 miles east of Henning, and then a short distance north on TN 207. (901) 738-5581. Hours: Daily 8a.m.-10p.m. Interpretive center hours: 8a.m.-4:30 p.m. Fort Pillow was overtaken by 1,500 Confederate soldiers on April 12, 1864. Half of the 500 men at the garrison were black soldiers and after their surrender many were killed. "Remember Fort Pillow!" became a the rallying cry that black troops used to steel themselves for battle and fight to the death. Remnants of the fort remain today, and the interpretative center offers an audio-visual program on the battle .

JACKSON

Casey Jones Home and Railroad Museum — Junction of I-40 and U.S. 45, bypass exit 80A. (901) 668-1222. Hours: Daily 8-8 June-Sept., rest of the year Mon.-Sat. 9-5, Sun.1-5. This museum honors the legendary locomotive engineer "Casey Jones" who was immortalized in the song written by Wallace Saunders, a black fireman who road aboard Jones' locomotive. The museum tells the story of the contribution blacks made to the development and running of the country's trains, from laying tracks to working as waiters in the dining cars. Along with railroad memorabilia, the museum houses the sister engine and tender to "Casey's Old 382."

Lane College—545 Lane Ave. (901) 424-4600. A National Historic Landmark that offers several interpretative displays of black culture on campus.

KNOXVILLE

Beck Cultural Exchange Center— 1927 Dandridge Ave., (615) 524-8461. Hours: Tues.-Sat. 10-6, Sun. by appointment only. Housed in an historic home, the center includes a library, museum and art gallery. Through photographic displays, documents, African-American art, and newspapers from the 1800's to the present, the center explains the first 100 years of black history in Knoxville.

Knoxville College—901 College St., (615) 524-6500. A National Historic Landmark founded in 1875, Knoxville College was one of the first black colleges established in Tennessee .

MEMPHIS

A. Schwab's Dry Goods Store —163 Beale St., (901) 523-9782. Hours: Mon.-Sat. 9-5. Founded in 1876, A. Schwab's is the oldest continuously operating business on Beale Street. The store's motto—"If you can't find it at Schwab's, you're better off without it"—is absolutely true. The three-story, wooden-floor store is jam-packed with everything from blue jeans to magic potions and blues records. An old-time record player continuously plays the tunes of Muddy Waters, Bessie Smith, and B.B. King. At one time Schwab's hosted one of the country's first blues radio programs called "Bluestown," which aired for an African-American audience from 1943 to

1947. Mr. Schwab still oversees the store and can often be found wandering around in his green apron.

Beale Street Historic District—off Riverside Drive in downtown Memphis. An entertainment district that sprawls several blocks east from the Mississippi River, Beale Street during the early 1900's was the center of night-life for the Memphis black community. It bustled with nightclubs, saloons, theaters, gambling houses and bordellos; for years whites were not allowed on the street at night. It was here that W.C. Handy played at the famous PeeWee's Saloon, other great performers debuted at various nightclubs, and the music known as blues was born when Handy played his hits "Memphis Blues," "Beale Street Blues," and "St. Louis Blues." Although many of the old haunts are gone, Beale Street today is a National Historic District with many restaurants, shops, and nightclubs, including B.B.'s Place, owned by the blues great, B.B. King.

Beale Street Tours—Memphis Visitors Center at 207 Beale St., (901) 526-4880. Hours: Mon.-Sat. 9-5, Sun. 11-4. Self-guided and escorted tours that focus on the black history, musical heritage and entertainment of Beale Street are offered during the day and at night.

Blues Hall—184 Beale St., (901) 528-0150. Hours vary, music Fri.-Sat. The small and smoky Blues Hall is a Memphis classic. Most performers here play a roots blues and the atmosphere is mellow and quiet. One of the bar's regulars is Mojo Buford, a harmonica player who used to perform with Muddy Waters.

Boss Ugly Bob's Tapes and Records —726 E. McLemore Ave., (901) 774-6400. Hours: Mon.-Sat. 8a.m.-10p.m., Sun. 10-7. A friendly Memphis hang-out that offers one of the best selections of R&B, blues and jazz records in the area.

Brittenum's Corner Lounge—1300 Airway Blvd. between midtown and east Memphis, (901) 458-2655. For the past 20 years, Brittenum's has offered a Sunday blues jam that attracts blues lovers from throughout the South.

Center for Southern Folklore —152 Beale St., (901) 525-3655. Hours: Mon.-Sat. 9-5:30, Sun. 1-5:30. This center has been documenting grass-roots southern culture through records, films, books, and festivals for almost 20 years. Its recently expanded location offers changing exhibits on music, walking tours of Beale Street, bus tours of Memphis and the Delta area, and a gift shop with an eclectic array of tapes, quilts, and handmade gifts.

Club Paradise —645 Georgia Ave., 10 minutes south of downtown, (901) 947-7144. Days and hours open vary. A large venue with a rowdy reputation, Club Paradise was the last Memphis establishment owned by the late blues lover Sunbeam Mitchell. Housed in a bowling alley with a funky decor, Club Paradise books major blues acts.

Full Gospel Tabernacle —787 Hale Road in Whitehaven, (901) 396-9192. Services at 11 a.m. on Sundays. The Reverend Al Green, known to most as the popular soul singer, took over the ministry six years ago. Although no one knows exactly when he will appear, curious fans seem to be more interested in the church than regular members. The octagonal building, equipped with a piano, drums, and tambourines, boasts a powerful sound when the Sunday music starts.

Graceland—3765 Elvis Presley Blvd., 1 1/2 miles south of Junction I-55, exit 5B, (901) 332-3322. Hours: Daily 8-6 June-August, 8-5 rest of the year. Closed Tuesdays, Nov.-Feb. The home of Elvis Presley, who adopted the sounds of black rhythm and blues, Graceland has become the Mecca for diehard Elvis fans from around the world. It offers tours of the mansion, his grave site, his private jets and car collection, and the Elvis Up Close Museum.

Green's Lounge — 2090 Person Ave. between midtown and east Memphis. (901) 274-9800. Hours vary. A neighborhood blues joint operated by Rose Green, Green's has been offering live music on weekends for over 15 years. Regulars include the Fieldstones, led by electric bass player Lois Brown and drummer Joe Hicks, and Evelyn Young, the sax player who worked with B.B. King for years. Although a casual place, patrons dress in their Sunday best and crowd the dance floor when the music begins.

Huey's —1927 Madison Ave. (901) 726-4372. Hours vary, live music usually Sunday afternoons. A big, casual and crowded bar that hosts the Midtown Jazzmobile, a group of top-rate Memphis players. A popular hang-out during the W.C. Handy Awards when visiting performers, including B.B. King, are likely to show up.

Ida B. Wells Plaque —First Baptist Beale Street Church, 379 Beale St., (901) 527-4832. On this site stands a plaque that honors Ida B. Wells, one of the first black women to publish a newspaper. The paper, "Free Speech," spoke out against the injustices endured by blacks in the early 1900s.

Mallory-Neely House —652 Adams Ave., (901) 523-1484. Hours: Tues.-Sun. 10-4. This preserved 25-room Italian-style Victorian mansion is where W.C. Handy performed during parties given by the owner of the home Mrs. Frances Neely. Handy and other black musicians played in a small, back room out of sight of the white guests. The home today is a museum.

Marmalder —153 Calhoun St., (901) 522-8800. Hours: Tues.-Sun. 6p.m.-varies. A rambling restaurant and club with a down-home atmosphere that features top-notch, Southern-style cooking. Live music Sun.-Thurs.

National Civil Rights Museum/Lorraine Motel—406 Mulberry St., (901) 521-9699. Hours: Mon.-Sat. 10-5, Sun. 1-5. This former motel building was where Dr. Martin Luther King, Jr., was murdered on April 4, 1968. The motel has been turned into a museum which offers a comprehensive view of the American civil rights movement through the use of audio-visual programs, interpretive exhibits, and sound-and-light displays. The contributions of King and other civil rights leaders are highlighted. A massive, steel sculpture honoring Dr. King entitled "The Mountain Top" stands at the north end of the Civic Center Plaza.

Mid-South Music and Heritage Festival — Hosted by the Center for Southern Folklore, 152 Beale St., (901) 525-3655. This annual festival held every July presents a three-day festival featuring music, arts and crafts, and southern cooking.

Mitchell Hotel —207 Beale St. Now a tourist information center, this was once a hotel and club operated by Andrew "Sunbeam" Mitchell who acted as a godfather to up-and-coming bluesmen. Mitchell, from the 1940's to the 1960's, took in many struggling musicians and gave them a place to stay and hot meal when they were down and out. Mitchell also ran several nightclubs on Beale Street where Count Bassie and Lionel Hampton played, helped Little Richard in his early years when he couldn't find work, and later served as a manager for B.B. King.

Monarch Club —340 Beale St. Once one of the classiest

clubs on Beale Street, the Monarch had mirrored walls and plush seats in its heydey. It was also known as the "Castle of Missing Men" because area ruffians who were killed on the streets were taken here and deposited in the undertaker's quarters in the back.

Old WDIA Building —2267 Central Ave. This brick building was where radio station WDIA was housed in the 1940's. B.B. King came here in 1948 hoping that the African-American station would give him a chance to air his music. King got a job as the station's "Pepticon Boy" singing commercials for a bogus health tonic. Eventually, he worked his way up to a full-fledged show of his own.

Palace Theater—318 Beale St., northeast corner of Hernando Street. No longer standing, the Palace Theater was once a center for the aspiring blues musicians of Beale Street. Its amateur shows gave breaks to B.B. King, Johnny Ace, and Bobby "Blue" Bland, and awarded each of them with a one-dollar prize.

Peabody Hotel —149 Union Ave., (901) 529-4000. Since the 1920's, the Peabody has been one of Memphis's most luxurious hotels. Listed on the National Register of Historic Places, the hotel hosted big band sounds during the 1930's and 1940's and catered to an elite, white clientele. In 1969 B.B. King was invited to perform at the Peabody giving him his first real break into white clubs. The hotel has a Memorabilia Room on the second floor which houses a display on the hotel's history. Mallard's, the hotel's old-world bar, offers blues on weekends.

Sun Studio—706 Union Ave., (901) 521-0664. Hours: Daily 10-6, tours every hour on the half hour. Called the birthplace of Rock'n'Roll, Sun Studio was opened by Sam Phillips in 1950 and for years was where many wannabe stars cut their first record. Among the artists to launch their recording careers from Sun were Elvis Presley, Jerry Lee Lewis, B.B. King, Rufus Thomas, Howlin' Wolf, Muddy Waters, Carl Perkins and Roy Orbison. In its early years anyone could cut a record at the studio for $4. These days, Sun Studio is a music museum that still operates as a recording studio at night.

Tom Lee Memorial —On the riverbank near Beale Street. A 30-foot high replica of the Washington Monument stands here in memory of Tom Lee, a black man who in 1925 rescued 32 people from a boating disaster on the Mississippi River.

W.C. Handy Awards —Sponsored by the Blues Foundation, 174 Beale St., (901) 527-BLUE. An awards ceremony and four-day conference held every November, the Handy Awards is a national blues award show that honors performers in 22 categories along with industry promoters, clubs, and societies noted for "keeping the blues alive. " Throughout the conference, the Memphis area hosts several special blues performances. The ceremony itself is open to the public with advance reservations required.

W.C. Handy's Home and the Handy Hall Blues Association —352 Beale St., (901) 527-2583. Hours: By appointment only. This small, shotgun house is where Handy lived when he wrote his most famous compositions: "Yellow Dog Blues," "Beale Street Blues," and "Ole Miss Blues." He also raised six children here before moving to New York to start his own publishing company. Although born in Florence, Alabama, William Christopher Handy spent much of his young life on Beale Street. The home houses a collection of Handy memorabilia including an old piano and photographs.

The Handy Hall Blues Association has its headquarters in the house.

W.C. Handy Park—Northwest corner of Beale and Hernando Streets. A bronze statue of William Christopher Handy, "Father of the Blues," overlooks the Beale Street he made famous. The park and statue are Memphis' tribute to the composer who died in 1958. Many musical events are held in the park throughout the summer months.

WDIA/1070 AM—112 Union St., (901) 529-4300. The country's first all-black-formatted radio station, WDIA has been broadcasting blues, gospel, oldies, news and talk since 1948. The station has a small museum that displays the history of its importance to the black community of Memphis, and features a special all-blues show on Saturday.

NASHVILLE

Battle of Nashville —A map showing the location of historic battle sites and markers can be obtained from the Metropolitan Historical Commission, Stahlman Building, Nashville; (615) 862-7970. Remnants of the old fort and trenches from the December, 1864 battle remain on the site where Union and Confederate forces fought. Eight black regiments formed a part of the Union army and the 13th U.S. Colored Infantry led the troops who got caught in a brutal barrage of musket fire. Although 25 percent of the black brigade was killed, the remainder managed to reach the summit of Overton Hill.

Carl Van Vechten Gallery of Fine Arts—Fisk University campus on the third floor of the library, (615) 329-8500. Hours: Tues.-Fri. 10-5, Sat.-Sun. 1-5. One of the finest African-American art galleries in the U.S., the Van Vechten houses the MacDonald Collection of African sculpture, contemporary black American art from the Alfred Stieglitz collection, and murals by Aaron Douglas.

Country Music Hall of Fame—4 Music Square East, 1 1/2 blocks south of exit 209B off I-40, (615) 256-1639. Hours: Daily, 8-8. June-Aug., rest of the year 9-5. A museum that honors white and black country performers. Exhibits include a hands-on look at the recording process, the history of country music, and a tribute to black musician DeFord Bailey who played his harmonica with white country bands between 1925 and 1941.

Fisk University —17th Avenue North, about two miles northwest of downtown Nashville, (615) 329-8500. Founded in 1866 for newly freed slaves, Fisk was called an institution "equal to the best in the country." The Fisk campus is doted with many historical buildings including the Little Theater which served as a hospital during the Civil War , and Jubilee Hall, named for the Fisk Jubilee Singers who have gained international acclaim for their plaintive spirituals. The campus library houses an extensive collection of material on blacks in America, the Caribbean and Africa, and holds several original manuscripts of W.E.B. DuBois and Langston Hughes. Its Meharry Medical School was the first black medical school in the U.S.

Greenwood Cemetery —1428 Elm Hill Pike, (615) 256-4395. A monument honoring country music great, De-Ford Bailey, was erected here in 1983.

Tennessee State Museum—505 Deaderick Street, in the lower level of the James Polk Cultural Center, (615) 741-2692. Hours: Mon.-Sat. 10-5, Sun. 1-5. Along with exhibits on general Tennessee history and the Battle of Nashville, the museum includes several displays on African-American history from slavery to the Civil War. A post-Civil War exhibit, with an audio-visual program, explains the hardships blacks endured during the days of Jim Crow.

Tennessee State University —350 John A. Merritt Blvd., (615) 320-3131. The 1937 founding of the first chapter of Alpha Kappa Mu, a black honorary society, is commemorated here as an historical landmark.

MISSISSIPPI

With its low-lying landscape laced with rivers, its rich, deep soil, and its long growing season, Mississippi was ideally suited to cotton-growing and hence to the development of a slave-dependent economy. Soon after the western part of the original Mississippi Territory created by Congress in 1789 achieved statehood as Mississippi in 1817 (the eastern part became the state of Alabama in 1819) land speculation and the growth of a plantation-based cotton economy led to an increasing slave population. Like South Carolina's, Mississippi's population soon comprised more blacks than whites.

In 1861, Mississippi seceded with the other Southern states to form the Confederate States of America. Many Mississippi slaves fought in the war on both sides. Wilson Brown was among those who managed to escape to North Carolina and enlist in the Union navy. In March 1863, the war sloop *Hartford* listed Brown as "contraband." While serving aboard the U.S.S. *Hartford*, in its Mobile bay engagement of August 5, 1864, Brown held his post, although some of the men at his station had been either killed or wounded. He was awarded the Medal of Honor for his bravery. Brown and many other black war dead are buried in Natchez National Cemetery.

Hiram R. Revels, a Methodist minister, recruited

blacks for the Union side during the war and served as chaplain for a Union regiment from Mississippi. During Reconstruction, he was the first black elected to the United States Senate. He later became president of Alcorn A&M, founded in 1871 in Lorman, Mississippi, and the first black land grant college in the United States.

Once Reconstruction had ended and Jim Crow laws had been introduced, white Mississippians looked to the coming of industry and railroads for economic salvation. But the sharecropping system that replaced slavery continued the economic dependence on farming and the economic interdependence of the races. Until about 1940, blacks continued to be in the majority. Not until the 1960s did industrial income surpass agricultural income.

Thus, Mississippi was fertile ground for the civil rights movement, spawning many of the activists and major events of that era. In 1962, 12,000 federal troops were ordered to Jackson to maintain order as riots erupted over the attempt by James Meredith, a 29-year-old black veteran, to enroll at the University of Mississippi.

In 1963, also in Jackson, Medgar Evers, a field secretary for the National Association for the Advancement of Colored People, was assassinated in the driveway of his home.

In 1964, in Philadelphia, Mississippi, three young civil rights workers, James Chaney, Michael Schwerner, and Andrew Goodman, were murdered. For the first time in the history of the South, members of the Ku Klux Klan were convicted of the killings. All three young men were working in a Student Nonviolent Coordinating Committee (SNCC) voting rights project called Mississippi Freedom Summer.

Fannie Lou Hammer, a former sharecropper from

Montgomery County, Mississippi, and others working with SNCC, formed the Mississippi Freedom Democratic Party (MEDP) that summer. At the Democratic national convention in Atlantic City that August, the MEDP delegates challenged the regular Mississippi delegation as not being representative of the people of Mississippi. Offered a compromise, Hammer refused. In 1965 *Mississippi* magazine named her one of six "Women of Influence" in the state.

In 1966 James Meredith was shot shortly after beginning a 220-mile voting rights pilgrimage from Memphis, Tennessee, to Jackson, Mississippi. Supporters from across the country took up the Meredith "March Against Fear," which ended in a huge rally in Jackson addressed by Meredith himself, Martin Luther King, Jr., and Stokely Carmichael.

MISSISSIPPI SITES

For general travel information contact the Mississippi Division of Tourism, P.O. Box 22825, Jackson, MS 39205. (800) 647-2290. A statewide heritage guide is being compiled. For a free brochure titled "Historic Natchez, the African-American Experience," write to the Natchez Visitors Bureau, 311 Liberty Rd., Natchez, MS 39120, or call (800) 647-6724.

BRICES CROSS ROADS

Brices Cross Roads National Battlefield Site—National Park Service, Mississippi I-370, six miles west of Baldwyn. (601) 842-1572. The 55th and 59th Colored Infantry Regiments and Battery F of the 2nd Colored Infantry Regiment demonstrated their courage here in a successful battle against Confederate cavalry in June of 1864.

CLARKSDALE

Blues Alley—Fourth St. Now a predominately black business district that is suffering from urban decay, this area was the heart of Clarksdale's entertainment strip when it was a major blues town from the 1930s to the 1950s. Born in this neighborhood were John Lee Hooker, Ike Turner, Little Junior Parker and Sam Cooke.

Delta Blues Museum—114 Delta Ave., in the downtown Carnegie Public Library building. (601) 624-4461. Hours: Mon.-Fri. 9-5. Although small and in cramped quarters, the Delta Blues Museum deserves to be praised. Established to increase the understanding and appreciation of the music that was born in the Mississippi Delta, the museum offers photographs, books, archives, videos, slide-and-sound shows, memorabilia and live performances. Also on display are a microphone used by Ike Turner and a sign from the Three Forks store behind which Robert Johnson supposedly died. With a grant from the National Endowment for the Humanities, the museum plans to expand in upcoming years.

Riverside Hotel—615 Sunflower Ave. (601) 624-9163. Formerly the Thomas Hospital, a black hospital where Bessie Smith was taken after her fatal accident, Riverside Hotel today is a modest establishment of some 25 rooms. During the 1940s when the hospital was transformed into a hotel, Sonny Boy Williamson, Robert Nighthawk, Kansas City Red, Jackie Brenston and others, called the hotel home. Their names are signed in the hotel's register. Ike Tuner and his band wrote and rehearsed his song "Rocket 88" at the Riverside.

Smitty's Red Top Lounge—377 Yazoo Ave. (601) 627-4421. Hours vary, call in advance. James "Smitty" Smith has been running this dilapidated but popular blues lounge for 25 years. Frank Frost and the Jelly Roll Kings posed for an album cover here once, and the place is known as far away as Europe. The music is sporadic but good.

Stackenhouse/Delta Record Mart—232 Sunflower Ave. (601) 627-2209. Hours: Mon.-Sat. 12-6. Run by Jim O'Neal, founder of *Living Blues* magazine, this record store and music center carries many 45s, 78s, LPs, CDs and cassettes of blues recordings by legendary greats and unknowns, as well as an original copy of *Living Blues* from its collection of back issues. It's also one of the best places for information on blues and blues tours in the Delta area, and serves as the base for Jim O'Neil's record label Rooster Blues Records.

Stovall Plantation/Muddy Waters Home—Oakridge Rd., eight miles from downtown. Not open to the public. The enormous Stovall Plantation was where Muddy Waters (McKinley Morganfield) grew up. The plantation once functioned as a city unto itself complete with cotton fields, an irrigation plant, general store, and church. Waters moved to the plantation when he was three-years-old with his grandmother. At the time, he was making music with anything and everything he could find. By the time he turned seven, he had already mastered the harmonica.

When Waters was 26 he drove a tractor for the plantation, and one day two folksong collectors from the Library of Congress came to Clarksdale to seek him out. They visited his home, which also served as a juke joint on weekends, and recorded him playing his guitar. A few months later Waters left Clarksdale and headed for Chicago. The Clarksdale Historical Society has plans to take part of the home and reconstruct it inside the Delta Blues Museum.

Wade Walton's Barber Shop—317 Issaquena Ave. Hours: Tues.-Sat. 10-6. Wade Walton is a Clarksdale institution. A barber who works in a bow tie and suspenders, Walton is also an accomplished musician who plays the harp and guitar. Born the sixteenth of 17 children, he started playing music as a young boy and recorded an album, "The Blues of Wade Walton." Occasionally, Walton plays his guitar for barbershop visitors near a sign that reads "Profanity will not be tolerated." He talks about the old days when Muddy Waters used to play nearby; and as a barber he remembers cutting the hair of Sunny Boy Williamson and Charlie Pride.

W.C. Handy's Home—Issaquena St. near Third St. Although no longer standing, this is the site of a house where W.C. Handy lived from 1903 to 1905. A plaque reads "In Clarksdale, W.C. Handy was influenced by Delta blues which he collected and later published."

WROX—Alcazar Hotel, corner of Third and Yazoo Sts. (601) 627-7343. Housed in a dark hall on the second-floor of the hotel, WROX is Clarksdale's only full-time, full-service radio station. It runs blues shows Mon.-Fri. 6-8p.m., and gospel shows 8-10 p.m. It is home base for Early Wright, one of the first black deejays in the South who has been playing blues shows since 1947. Wright's deep voice has been a soothing sound to listeners for years and his smooth-flowing shows are a Mississippi Delta radio staple.

CORINTH

Corinth National Cemetery—1551 Horton St. (601) 286-5782. Although during the Civil War many black Mississippi soldiers were buried in trenches, men of the Federal 14th, 40th, 106th, 108th and 111th Colored Infantry Regiments were buried here at Corinth Cemetery. An historic marker at the junction of US 45 and SR 2 describes the Battle of Corinth.

DOCKERY

Dockery Farms—Hwy. 8 between Cleveland and Ruleville. Dockery was once a huge plantation where some music historians say Delta Blues was born. What remains of the plantation is the Dockery Baptist Church, and a faded sign on a wooden barn that reads "Dockery Farms established in 1895." Early bluesman Charley Patton once lived here, as did his teacher Henry Sloan who was known to be playing the blues as far back as 1897. Patton lived in the Dockery area almost all his life and many of his songs reflect his days there. His song "Pea Vine Blues" was written about the Dockery railroad, nicknamed the "Pea Vine" because of its complicated route.

GREENVILLE

Delta Blues Festival—Organized by MACE, 119 S. Theobold St. (601) 335-3523. Always the third weekend in September, this festival is the biggest annual blues event in the country.

Perry's Flowing Fountain—816 Nelson St. (601) 335-9836. Hours vary, phone ahead. This cozy little blues club, decorated with Christmas lights, is owned by Perry Payton. Payton worked as a mortician, and was friends with all the blues greats—Ray Charles, B.B. King, Little Junior Parker, Howlin' Wolf—when they were just getting started. Many of them who are still alive drop in whenever they're in town. Part of the club is called Annie Mae's Cafe, which is noted in a Little Milton song.

Playboy Club —928 Nelson St. (601) 378-9924. Hours vary. Owned and operated by Roosevelt "Booba" Barnes, one of the best blues performers in the Delta today; this run-down club offers fine blues on weekends to a usually jam-packed crowd.

GREENWOOD

Cottonlandia Museum—2 3/4 miles west on US 82W bypass. (601) 453-0925. Hours: Tues.-Fri. 9-5, Sat.-Sun. 2-5. This museum has exhibits on the inhabitants of the Mississippi River Delta region from pre-Columbian times to the present. It also offers an exhibit on the history of cotton production in the Delta, which became one of the more profitable endeavors in the South due to the labor of thousands of black field hands. Included in the exhibits are original farm tools made and used by slaves.

Florewood River Plantation State Park—Two miles west of Greenwood and south of US 82 and US 49E. (601) 455-3821 or 455-3822. Hours: Tues.-Sat. 9-noon and 1-5, Sun. 1-5, open early March through early November. A recreated antebellum plantation that offers demonstrations of nineteenth-century crafts and trades, most of which were performed by plantation slaves. The grounds include a cotton museum complete with a restored cotton gin that explains the history of cotton— from the invention of the cotton gin in 1793 by Eli Whitney to the production over 6,000,000 bales a year by Southern slaves. Costumed tour guides explain what life was like on a plantation during the 1800s.

HOLLY SPRINGS

Rust College —On MS 78. (601) 252-4661. Established in 1866 as Shaw University for the education of freed slaves, Rust College was renamed in 1890 to honor

Richard Sutton Rust, Methodist clergyman, educator and abolitionist.

INDIANOLA

Indianola—A small, riverfront town with a tiny Main Street, Indianola is the birthplace of B.B. King. The town has a B.B. King Street and on the corner of Second and Church Streets are King's handprints stamped into the city sidewalk. King returns to his hometown every year in June to give a free concert at Fletcher Park, and sponsors a local baseball team, the B.B. Kings.

JACKSON

Ace Records—209 W. Capitol St. Founded in 1955 by Johnny Vincent, the Ace record label was mostly known for rock-and-roll, but the label also recorded a few R&B artists such as Earl King and Frankie Ford. Vincent's Ace Records went out of business in the 1960s, but there are currently plans to bring it back to life.

Farish Street Festival—Farish St. (601) 355-2787. This annual September festival is a return to the days when Farish Street was the hub of Mississippi's black political and cultural life. Tours of the historic district during the festival feature thirteen landmarks.

Jackson State University—1400 John R. Lynch St. (601) 968-2121. Founded in Natchez in 1877 and moved to Jackson in 1882, this university was started with 20 black scholars. Today, it has a student body of 7,000. Historic portraits, and a rare book collection are housed in the Founder's Room of the campus library.

Medgar Evers/Mississippi Homecoming—(601) 378-3141. Every June Jackson hosts a week-long tribute to the works of civil rights activist Medgar Evers. The tribute is sponsored by blues artist B.B. King, actor and country musician Kris Kristofferson, and Charles Evers, brother of the slain activist.

Mississippi State Historical Museum—On State and Capitol Sts. in the Old State Capitol building. (601) 359-6920. Hours: Mon.-Fri. 8-5, Sat.-9:30-4:30, Sun. 12:30-4:30. A chronological display on Mississippi's history beginning with Desoto's exploration of the territory through the Civil War and Reconstruction period, and up to the civil rights movement.

Mt. Helm Baptist Church—300 E. Church St., southwest corner of Lamar and Church Sts. (601) 353-3981. Formed in 1835, this church is the oldest black religious body in the city.

Queen of Hearts—2243 Martin Luther King, Jr., Dr. (601) 366-2311. Music begins at 11 p.m. on weekends. This popular, neighborhood blues joint is also a favorite barbecue restaurant that serves mouth-watering chicken and ribs from an outdoor grill.

Smith Robertson Museum and Cultural Center—528 Bloom St. (601) 960-1457. Hours: Mon.-Fri. 9-5, Sat. 9-12, Sun. 2-5. Housed in Jackson's first public school building for blacks, this is the first museum devoted to black culture and history in the state of Mississippi. It is named for Smith Robertson, a former slave who moved to Jackson in 1874, and devoted his entire life to black education. The museum offers displays on the history, life and culture of black Mississippians. Exhibits include an interpretation of Jackson's Farish Street Historic District, the contributions of blacks to education, business and politics; and the work of black folk artists and craftsmen.

Trumpet Records—309 N. Farish St. No longer in existence. Founded in 1950 by furniture and record saleswoman Lillian McMurry, Trumpet Records recorded several early blues artists including Sonny Boy Williamson. McMurry, her brother and a friend searched all over the Delta to track down Williamson and finally found him in a little shack. After a friendly chat, she signed him and produced one of his earliest records.

LORMAN

Alcorn State University—US 61, south of Port Gibson at the MS 552 junction. (601) 877-6114. Alcorn State University is the first black land grant college in the U.S. The university's former president was Hiram Revels, a black gentleman who served as a state senator before becoming a U.S. senator in 1870. In addition to being an astute politician, Revels was also an educator and minister who completed the unexpired term of Jefferson Davis, the former president of the defeated Confederate States of America. The historic campus chapel was built in 1838.

Windsor Plantation Ruins—10 miles northwest of Lorman on MS 552 in the Port Gibson area. Built in 1860, Windsor was once one of the most beautiful plantation mansions in the South. Over 600 slaves labored on the four-story building which was destroyed by fire in 1890. Today, only the 23 columns that supported the house remain.

MOUND BAYOU

Mound Bayou—On US 61. One of the largest black towns in the U.S., Mound Bayou was settled in July 1887 by ex-slaves who hoped to establish a community where they could enjoy social, economic and political freedom.

Isaiah Thornton Montgomery Home—West Main St. Not open to the public. Listed on the National Register of Historic Places, this home once belonged to Isaiah Thornton Montgomery, one of the founders of Mound Bayou. Montgomery was one of the few black members of the 1890 state convention.

NATCHEZ

Carriage House Restaurant—401 High St. on the grounds of Stanton Hall. (601) 445-5151. Hours: 11:00a.m.-2:30p.m. A Southern hospitality kind of place that features fried chicken, baked ham, tiny biscuits, and an array of Cajun dishes.

Dunleith—84 Homochitto St. (601) 446-8500. Hours: Mon.-Sat. 9-5, Sun. 12:30-5. A Greek Revival-style mansion, Dunleith is where John R. Lynch served as a house servant. Lynch, a former slave with little formal education, was one of the most influential political voices in post-Civil War American history. He became Speaker of the House in Mississippi in 1872, and in 1873 was elected to the U.S House of Representatives. He later went on to serve as president of the Capital Savings Bank in Washington, D.C., the first black bank in the U.S., and was author of the book *The Facts of Reconstruction*. Today, Dunleith remains in its original condition complete with period antiques.

Evans-Bontura-Smith House—106 Broadway. Not open to the public. The Smith House was once the luxurious home of Robert Smith, a free black who operated a prosperous taxi business in pre-Civil War Natchez.

Holy Family Catholic Church—16 Orange Ave. This is Mississippi's oldest black Catholic church.

Mostly African Market—St. Catherine and McCabe Sts. (601) 442-5448. Hours: Wed.-Sat 1-5 and July and August by appointment only. Sponsored by Project Southern

Cross, this market housed in an antebellum Gothic cottage features a gallery with African and African-American arts and crafts.

Natchez Museum of Afro-American History and Culture—307 Market St. (601) 442-0199. Hours: Wed. 1-5, Sat. 10-5. A museum dedicated to the black history and culture of Natchez.

Natchez National Cemetery—61 Cemetery Rd. At the end of the Civil War 2,484 black soldiers were buried on this site. Among the well-known were landsmen Wilson Brown and seaman John Lawson, both awarded the Medal of Honor during the Civil War. Hiram Revels, black statesmen and president of Alcorn College, is also buried here.

Richard N. Wright Marker—Bluff Park on Broadway near the bandstand. Richard Wright, one of the world's most revered black literary figures, was born near Natchez in 1908. The son of sharecroppers, Wright gained international acclaim when he published his shocking and poignant books on the black experience in America, *Native Son* and *Black Boy.* Wright later moved to France where he died in 1960.

Rose Hill Baptist Church—607 Madison St. This is Mississippi's oldest black Baptist church.

Slave Market Site—St. Catherine and Liberty Rds. Like the river landing on Silver Street, this was one of the many slave auction sites in Natchez. Due to the growth of the cotton industry in the Mississippi Delta after the War of 1812, the Natchez area became one of the busiest slave trading posts in the South.

William Johnson House—210 State St. Not open to the public. William Johnson was a free black resident of Natchez who published a diary that remains today the most complete account of the life of a free black in the antebellum South. As part of the free black aristocracy of Natchez, Johnson had business dealings with the white community, and owned slaves of his own.

Zion Chapel A.M.E. Church—338 Martin Luther King, Jr., St. This church was acquired in 1868 by Zion Chapel, whose minister at the time, Hiram Revels, became the first black U.S. senator.

OXFORD

Isom Place—1003 Jefferson Ave. (601) 234-3310. By appointment only. Constructed entirely of native timber and handcrafted by Indian and slave labor, this building is a classic example of planter-type architecture.

University of Mississippi Center for the Study of Southern Culture — Farley Hall. (601) 232-7753. Hours: Tues.-Sat. 10-4, Sun. 1-4. A research center that focuses on Southern music, literature and folklife. It contains the Blues Archives, which houses B.B. King's personal collection of 10,000 records. The University of Mississippi is remembered for the 1962 showdown that occurred here when James Meredith, a young black, attempted to register for classes at the formerly all-white school, bringing about an intervention by President John F. Kennedy who sent 3,000 federal troops to Oxford on Meredith's behalf. The dramatic confrontation took place at the campus's Lyceum Building.

PHILADELPHIA

Freedom Summer Murders—Information about the deaths can be found on an historical marker at Mt. Zion Methodist Church on a country road about one mile off MS 482, five miles northeast of Philadelphia. In June 1964, the murders of three voting rights activists who fell victim to a Ku Klux Klan conspiracy provoked national outrage and led to the first successful federal prosecution of a civil rights case in Mississippi.

PINEY WOODS

Piney Woods Country Life School—Hwy 49 South. (601) 845-2214. This black boarding school was established in 1909 by Dr. Laurence C. Jones. Its curriculum, work program and Christian philosophy seek to "educate head, heart and hands."

TOUGALOO

Tougaloo College—500 County Line Road off of I-55. (601) 977-7700. Tougaloo College is an accredited liberal arts college with an enrollment of 940. It was built on the grounds of a former plantation in 1869 by the American Missionary Association. At the time, the educational policy at Tougaloo was that black students should be educated not to "know" their place but to "find" it. There were many who thought that the college was a "hotbed of impudent blacks." Tougaloo College became the heart of the Mississippi civil rights movement during the late 1950s and early 1960s, when many students took part in peaceful demonstrations and sit-ins. Many of the campus's historic buildings are preserved.

TUPELO

Tupelo National Battlefield—West Main St. off MS 6, one mile west of the intersection of I-6 and US 45; one mile east of the Natchez Trace Parkway. (601) 842-1572. Markers, maps, and monuments honoring both Union and Confederate armies describe the Battle of Tupelo, fought here by both black and white units. Tupelo was the site of the last major Civil War battle fought in

Mississippi. The battle at Brices Cross Road, to the north of Tupelo, in which black troops were engaged, took place in June 1864. Some of those same black troops from the 59th, as well as the 61st and 68th Colored Infantry Regiments, also participated in the battle of Tupelo in July 1864. After the black soldiers displayed steadfast courage, the commanding general asked that they be included in the forces used to capture Mobile, Alabama.

TUTWILER

Sonny Boy Williamson's Grave—Adjacent to the Whitfield Church, just outside Tutwiler. Although the gravestone of the legendary blues musician is quite large, it is very difficult to find because it is usually hidden beneath an overgrowth of vegetation. A collection of harmonicas, left by visiting fans, adorns the stone.

Parchman Penitentiary—Hwy 49W between Tutwiler and Drew. Many of the Mississippi Delta's famed blues performers were incarcerated at Parchman Penitentiary for crimes both big and small, and the prison has been celebrated in several of their songs including Bukka White's "Parchman Farm Blues." White was involved in a barroom brawl that left one man dead and rather than face charges, he fled to Chicago. Then one night while recording a song at a studio, a Mississippi sheriff deputy showed up, arrested him and brought him back to Tutwiler where he served time at Parchman. But White persevered and actually wound up recording material for the National Library of Congress' Archive of American Folk Song while in prison. Today, Parchman remains a state penitentiary surrounded by barren fields.

VICKSBURG

Bethel A.M.E. Church—805 Monument St. This was the

site of first African Methodist Episcopal Church built in 1864, and the first Negro Masonic lodge in Mississippi in 1875. The present church was built in 1912.

Blue Room—Corner of Clay and Mulberry Sts. No longer in operation. Once one of the best clubs around, featuring the finest that jazz and blues had to offer: Louis Armstrong, Dinah Washington, Louis Jordon, and Count Basie. The Blue Room from 1937 to 1972 was a legendary club owned by Tom Wince, a half-black, half-Jewish man who boasted of having had thirteen wives.

Duff Green Mansion—1114 First East St. (601) 636-6968 or (800) 992-0037. Hours: daily from 9-5. This lovely three-story mansion was constructed by skilled slave labor and once served as a hospital for Confederate and Union soldiers during the Civil War. It currently operates as a bed-and-breakfast inn, but offers tours of the historic home.

Old Court House Museum—1008 Cherry St. (601) 636-0741. Hours: Mon.-Sat. 8:30-4:30, Sun. 1:30 p.m.-4:30. Vicksburg's most historic building, constructed by slaves in 1858, has hosted such great Americans as Jefferson Davis, Theodore Roosevelt, John Breckinridge, Booker T. Washington, William McKinley, and U.S. Grant. Here the U.S. flag was raised and the Confederate lowered on July 4, 1863. Museum artifacts tell the Vicksburg story along with an exhibit on local blacks and their contribution to the community. The restored courtroom's original iron grillwork was likely produced by black craftsmen.

U.S.S. *Cairo* Museum—Opposite the National Cemetery entrance. (601) 636-7827. Hours: daily 8-7, June-Aug.; rest of year 8-5. A museum that displays the artifacts recovered from the Union ship *Cairo*, which was sunk north of Vicksburg in 1862. Many black laborers served on the *Cairo* as crew. The visitor center offers a movie of the Vicksburg campaign, and exhibits on what the siege was like for both soldiers and civilians. A self-guided tour takes visitors past the sites of forts, trenches, artillery emplacements, and scenes of combat.

Vicksburg National Military Park and Cemetery—Clay St. off US 80, within one mile of I-20. (601) 636-0583. The cemetery lies in the north end of the park and is entered via Connecting and Union Avenues. This 1,700-acre park is the site where in 1863, for 47 days, the Union army took hold of Vicksburg. Many Vicksburg residents hid from the shelling in nearby caves. Several members of the black regiments who took part in the siege are buried at the cemetery along with over 17,000 Civil War soldiers.

GEORGIA

With its far-reaching cotton fields, white columned mansions, and historic coastal towns, Georgia is saturated with Deep South sentiment. It is also full of pride and sadness, for its most famous native born son, Martin Luther King, Jr.

In its earliest days, Georgia started out as a conservative colony. Both rum and the importation of slaves were forbidden. The original settlers wanted to bring their own European servants, and felt that the onslaught of African slaves might be a threat to their peaceful existence. But when the need for massive amounts of laborers became apparent in the 1740s, this no-slave policy was abandoned, and the rum started flowing.

In the early 1800s many of Georgia's Native American Indians were forced off their land and out of the state to make way for the cotton that would soon become king. Plantations spread throughout the state, and so did slavery. By the 1850s, Georgia was the world's greatest cotton producer. Just prior to the Civil War, about 60,000 families in Georgia owned a total of 500,000 slaves. Strong, muscular male slaves were sold at the auction block for about $1,800 a piece. Most of the state's great plantation houses, classic examples of Greek Revival and Victorian architecture, were built with the brute strength of these slaves.

After resisting anti-slavery measures, Georgia seceded from the Union in 1861 and sided with the Confederacy. When Union forces under General Sherman raged through the state, Georgia's economy was left in shambles.

Although slavery was abolished in 1865, much of the Old South "master mentality" remained. In 1868 twenty-seven black members of state legislature were expelled. In 1908 blacks were disenfranchised by the enforcement of poll taxes and literacy tests.

By 1945, federal court decisions opened Georgia primaries to blacks which resulted in a large increase in voting by blacks in the 1950s. In 1954, token desegregation began, but it encountered massive resistance. The 1960s were a potent time for civil rights demonstrations throughout the state. Martin Luther King, Jr., made several Georgia cites targets for his protests. In 1966, Lester Maddox was chosen as governor. Maddox was notorious for his violent resistance to the desegregation of his own Atlanta restaurant.

In the late 1960s, federal courts ordered Georgia to create a racially balanced school system. Jimmy Carter was elected governor in 1971 and declared the era of racial discrimination as over, and went on to appoint blacks to state offices. In 1972 Georgia elected its first black congressman since Reconstruction. In 1973 Atlanta elected its first black mayor. By the mid-1970s, blacks had become an influential voting block in the state.

Today, the state boasts several outstanding institutions of higher education that have nurtured numerous black achievers. Among them are Clark Atlanta University, Moorehouse College, and Spelman College.

Eatonton, southeast of Atlanta, is noted for being the home of Joel Chandler Harris. Chandler wrote about the

Old South with slave cabin dwellings in his stories about Uncle Remus and his famous critters Br'er Rabbit and Br'er Fox while living in Eatonton. Alice Walker, Pulitzer Prize-winning author of *The Color Purple*, was also born in Eatonton. Macon, in the center of the state, was the hometown of musical greats Lena Horne, Little Richard, and Otis Redding.

But the most revered birthsite in the state remains in Atlanta. It was in the city's Sweet Auburn Historic District that Martin Luther King, Jr., was born in 1929. Today, the Martin Luther King, Jr., National Historic Site on Auburn Avenue is a national shrine to the late civil rights hero. It attracts thousands of visitors a year who come to see King's birthhome and museum, archive center, and marble tombstone which reads "FREE AT LAST, FREE AT LAST, THANK GOD ALMIGHTY I'M FREE AT LAST."

GEORGIA SITES

For general travel information contact the Georgia Department of Industry, Trade and Tourism, 285 Peachtree Center Ave., Suite 1000, Atlanta, GA 30303. (404) 656-3590.

ALBANY

Albany Museum of Art—311 Meadowlark Dr. (912) 439-8400. Hours: Tues.-Sun. 12-5. Houses one of the largest, permanent collections of African and African-American art in the South.

ANDERSONVILLE

Andersonville National Historic Site—On GA 49, 10 miles north of Americus. (912) 924-0343. Hours: daily

8:30-5. A former Confederate prison constructed in 1864, the Andersonville site is dedicated to Civil War prisoners and American prisoners of war. It was here that prisoner Corporal James Henry Gooding, a member of the all-black 54th Massachusetts Volunteers, was held captive and eventually died. But before he died, Gooding wrote a letter to President Lincoln protesting the fact that black soldiers received lower pay than white soldiers. Following Gooding's death, the U.S. Congress passed a bill authorizing equal pay for all soldiers. The site contains remnants of the prison stockade, escape tunnels, a museum, and information center.

ATLANTA

African-American Panoramic Experience (APEX) Museum—135 Auburn Ave. N.E. (404) 521-2739. Hours: Tues., Thurs.-Sat. 10-5; Wed. 10-6; Sun. 1-5. Part of the Sweet Auburn Historic District, the museum boasts an impressive collection of art and artifacts relating to black life in America. Exhibits include a 1905 trolley car, a reproduction of a 1920s black-owned Georgia drugstore, and audio-visual presentations narrated by Cicily Tyson and Julian Bond.

Atlanta Life Insurance Headquarters—100 Auburn Ave. N.E. (404) 659-2100. Hours: Mon.-Thurs. 8-4:30. Founded in 1927 by Alonzo Herndon of Auburn Ave,, this black insurance company has a permanent exhibition on its history in its office lobby.

Atlanta University Center—111 James P. Brawley Dr. S.W. (404) 522-8980. A world-renowned consortium of historically black institutions which have educated and inspired black leaders for more than a century.

Blues Harbor—Underground Atlanta. (404) 524-3001. Hours: Mon.-Thurs. 6p.m.-1a.m., Fri.-Sun. 6p.m.-2a.m.

An up-scale blues and jazz bar with fine food. National acts perform nightly.

Clark Atlanta University—James P. Brawley Dr. at Fair St. (404) 880-8000. A predominantly black university that was formed through the consolidation of Atlanta University, founded in 1865, and Clark College, founded in 1869.

Dante's Down the Hatch—3380 Peachtree Rd. N.E. (404) 266-1600. Hours: Mon.-Fri. 4p.m.-midnight, Sat. 4p.m.-1a.m., Sun. 5p.m.-11p.m. An Atlanta institution, Dante's has been called the best jazz club in the city. Light meals are available with music nightly.

Decatur Street—Near Peachtree St. where Georgia State University is now located. It was on Decatur St. that Atlanta's black nightlife thrived during the early 1900s. At the time, the street was dotted with saloons, piano bars, pool halls, and black theaters.

Ebenezer Baptist Church—407 Auburn Ave. N.E. (404) 688-7263. Located near the birthplace of Martin Luther King, Jr., it was here that King shared the pulpit with his father for many years. Services still provided.

Hammonds House Galleries and Resource Center of African-American Art—503 Peeples St. S.W. (404) 752-8215. Hours: Tues.-Fri. 10-6, Sat-Sun. 1-5. A national center for the exhibition, preservation, and research of African-American arts and related materials. The gallery collection, located in a nineteenth-century Victorian home, includes African-American art as well as art from Africa and Haiti. Tours, lectures, and cultural programs are offered.

The Herndon Home—587 University Place N.W. (404) 727-6013. Hours: Tues.-Sat. 10-4. Adjacent to the Atlanta University Center, the Herndon Home stands as a testimonial to the business genius of Americans of African descent. A Beaux Arts classical mansion, designed and built in 1910 by former slave Alonzo Herndon who founded the Atlanta Life Insurance Company, features a history of the Herndon family along with the family's antique furniture, Roman and Venetian glass, photographs, and art.

Martin Luther King, Jr. Birthhome—501 Auburn St. (404) 331-5190. Hours: daily 10-5 June-August, the rest of the year 10-3:30. Located in the Sweet Auburn Historic District. Guided tours of Dr. King's home and surrounding area are available.

Martin Luther King, Jr., Center For Non-Violent Social Change—449 Auburn Ave. N.E. (404) 524-1956. Hours: daily 9-5:30. Located in the Freedom Hall Complex, the center includes Dr. King's marble crypt, a chapel, reflecting pool, exhibit area, and archives center which houses personal belongings and manuscripts of Dr. King.

Martin Luther King, Jr., National Historic Site—522 Auburn Ave. N.E. (404) 681-2800. Hours: daily 10-4:30. This preservation district includes Dr. King's birthplace, church, and gravesite. Guided walking tours of the area begin at the information center.

Martin Luther King, Jr., Week—Late January. (404) 526-8940. A week-long city-wide celebration commemorating the birthday of Dr. Martin Luther King,Jr. Activities include church services, concerts, lectures, a parade, and Freedom Trail March.

Mary Mac's Ltd.—224 Ponce De Leon Ave. (404) 876-6604. Hours: Mon.-Fri. 11a.m.-4p.m., Sat.-Sun. 5p.m.-8p.m. A local favorite for Southern home-cooking. The reasonably priced menu includes fried chicken, turnip greens, and cornbread.

Moorhouse College—830 Westview Dr. S.W. (404) 681-2800. Founded in 1867 for ex-slaves. Located on the campus are the Martin Luther King International Chapel and statue of Dr. King.

Morris Brown College—643 Martin Luther King, Jr., Dr. N.W. (404) 525-7831. Founded in 1881 as a co-educational college for blacks. The college's Ruth Hall Hodges Art Gallery (Hours: Mon.-Fri. 9-12) features a collection of African and African-American art.

Pascal's Restaurant and Lounge—830 Martin Luther King, Jr., Dr. S.W. (404) 577-3150. Hours: Mon.-Fri. 7:30a.m.-midnight, Sat.-Sun. 2p.m.-2:30a.m. Within walking distance of the Herndon Home, Pascal's specializes in home-style Southern cooking with jazz andblues nightly.

Royal Peacock—186 Auburn Ave. Although no longer in operation, this former theater opened in 1949 was a cultural center that once hosted nationally acclaimed performers like Nat King Cole, Cab Calloway, and Sam Cooke. The theater marquee and neon sign are still intact, and a barbershop now occupies the ground floor.

Spelman College—350 Spelman Lane S.W. (404) 681-3643. Founded in 1881, most of the buildings on campus are considered historic landmarks.

Stone Mountain Park—Hwy. 78, northeast of Atlanta (404) 498-5600. Hours: daily 6 a.m.-midnight; closed Christmas. A 3,200-acre recreational park. In addition to numerous outdoor activities, the park features the Antebellum Plantation, a collection of historic buildings moved here from other areas of the state, that includes authentically furnished slave cabins.

Sweet Auburn Historic District—Auburn Ave. (404) 524-6754. Once called the "richest Negro street in the world," Auburn Avenue was the hub of black enterprise in Atlanta from 1890-1930. The nation's oldest black daily paper the *Atlanta Daily World* was founded here in 1928.

AUGUSTA

Springfield Baptist Church—114 12th St. (404) 724-1056. One of the oldest, independent black Baptist congregations in the nation founded in 1787. Services still held.

Yerby Home—1112 8th St. Black author Frank Yerby lived here until his graduation from Paine College in 1937. Not open to the public.

CARTERSVILLE

Nobel Hill—2371 Joe Frank Harris Pkwy. (404) 382-3392. Hours: Tues.-Sat. 8-12, 1-4. A black history museum and cultural center housed in the former Noble Hill Rosenwald School, one of the first schools in northwest Georgia dedicated to the education of black children.

CUTHBERT

Fletcher Henderson's Home—1016 Andrew St. approximately 120 miles south of Atlanta. This one-story Victorian home, built in 1888, was where noted jazz musician Fletcher Henderson was raised. Although not open to the public, the home is listed on the NationalRegister of Historic Places.

EATONTON

Hometown of Alice Walker—Eatonton is the hometown of noted author Alice Walker whose book *The Color Purple* won the Pultizer Prize and the National Book Award in 1983.

Uncle Remus Museum—US 441 South. (404) 485-6856.

Hours: Mon.-Sat. 10-noon and 1-5, Sun. 2-5. Closed Tues. Oct.-Mar. A log cabin museum that honors Joel Chandler Harris, author of the well-known Uncle Remus stories. The museum portrays the slave cabin setting of his folktales with authentic furnishings. A park and picnic area are adjacent to the property.

LOCUST GROVE

Shoal Creek Baptist Church—364 O'Griffin Rd. (404) 957-6220. Dr. Martin Luther King, Jr., was pastor for a time here. Services still held.

MACON

Harriet Tubman Historical and Cultural Museum—340 Walnut St. (912) 743-8544. Hours: Mon.-Fri. 10-5, Sat. 2-5. Named for the dauntless woman who escaped slavery and then risked her life to lead hundreds of other African-Americans to freedom on the Underground Railroad. The museum features exhibits on black artists, African arts and crafts, portraits of Harriet Tubman,and a library of black history.

RESACA

Confederate Cemetery—Part of the Blue Gray Trail, off I-75. This cemetery is dedicated to Mary Green, a young girl, who with her sister Pryatt and two former slaves buried two fallen soldiers in their flower garden.

SAVANNAH

First African Baptist Church—23 Montgomery St. (912) 233-6597. Founded in 1777 at Brompton Plantation, this church was built at its present site on Savannah's Franklin Square in 1832. One of the first Baptist churches in America to be built of brick, historians say that in its early years escaped slaves hid in a tunnel underneath the floor.

King-Tisdell Cottage—514 E. Huntington St. (912) 234-000. Hours: Mon.-Fri. 10:30-4:30, Sat.-Sun. 1-4. An architectural gem furnished with turn-of-the-century antiques, this cottage museum is considered Savannah's center for black heritage. On display are slave handbills, African weapons, baskets, art, and carvings. The museum sponsors Savannah's Negro Heritage Tour, which begins at the cottage and continues on to seventeen historic sites. A minimum 24-hour advance reservation is required.

Laurel Grove Cemetery—802 W. Anderson St. (912)651-6772. Hours: Mon.-Fri. 7-5, Sat.-Sun. 11-4. Another of Savannah's historical sites, this cemetery is a final resting place for many black soldiers who died in theCivil War, as well as many prominent African-Americans of this century.

Second African Baptist Church—123 Houston St. (912) 233-6163. This historic church, built in 1859, was the site where General Sherman read the Emancipation Proclamation, promising displaced slaves 40 acres of land and a mule. It is also where Dr. Martin Luther King, Jr., delivered his "I Have a Dream" sermon before going on to give his civil rights address at the Lincoln Memorial in Washington, D.C.

FLORIDA

The sunny, sub-tropical peninsula that is Florida has been, and continues to be, a place known to offer a new life to runaways from the North. Although the first black in recorded history to set foot on Florida land was a man known as Little Steven who accompanied the Spanish conquistador Narvaez to Tampa Bay in 1528, for the most part, the blacks of early Florida history were runaway slaves fleeing their masters in Georgia and the Carolinas.

During the 1700s and 1800s, thousands of slaves journeyed southward to Florida's vast swamplands which at the time had more alligators than people. In 1738, the settlement of Fort Mose two miles north of St. Augustine was established by the Spaniards for escaped slaves. The black men and women who lived in Fort Mose, the first free black community in the United States, fought with the Spaniards and Native Indians against their former masters.

By the mid-1830s, about 1,500 blacks lived with the Seminole Indian tribe of Florida, only 200 of them as slaves. Many blacks found that the Seminoles treated them better than the whites, and adopted the Indian language and way of life. During the Seminole Wars, many blacks fought alongside the Seminoles against the white settlers. During the late 1800s, when the mistreatment of the Indians by the whites intensified, some of the black Seminoles remained with the tribe and moved with them to western parts of the country.

In 1839 Florida joined the Union as a slave state. By the 1840s white Florida landowners became frightened by the notion of free blacks, and passed laws that required all free blacks to have white guardians, and all free black sailors to remain on their ships while in Florida ports. By 1860, there were over 60,000 slaves living on north Florida plantations and a man's wealth was measured by the number of slaves he owned. Florida indeed established itself early on as a part of the segregationist South.

When the Civil War began, Florida sided with the Confederate states and about 1,200 free blacks joined the Union Army. The state lost pivotal battles, fought by both whites and blacks, at Jacksonville and Olustee.

During Reconstruction, Florida was seen as a liberal state due to the fact that nineteen blacks served in the state legislature. In 1868 a black man named Jonathan Gibbs served as Florida's secretary of state. But progress following Reconstruction was slow, and until the Civil Rights Act of 1964, blacks in Florida continued to live under severe repression and prejudice.

In 1873 Josiah T. Walls was elected as the state's first black congressman. In the late 1800s, many blacks from the Bahamas settled in Key West and the newly incorporated city of Miami. Miami's first registered voter was a black man. In 1889 the central Florida town of Eatonville advertised itself as a "Negro city governed by Negroes" and invited blacks from around the country to come and live there.

By 1900, blacks constituted 44 percent of Florida's population, but the percentage of blacks began to dwindle in the years that followed when white Northerners started to migrate to the state. In 1901 noted black author and folklorist Zora Neale Hurston was born in the central Florida town of Eatonville. In 1904, Bethune-Cookman College was founded by black educator Mary McLeod Bethune in Daytona.

During the 1930s, the Miami neighborhood of Overtown became known on the national scene as a strip of jazz clubs and theaters called the Great Black Way. It was here that jazz greats Cab Calloway, Billie Holiday and Louis Armstrong who performed at Miami Beach hotels but were not allowed to stay the night, came to unwind. Until 1947, blacks were not allowed on Miami Beach after dark.

The civil rights movement in Florida gained momentum in 1951 when Harry T. Moore, president of the Florida NAACP, was killed by white racists at his home in the small east coast town of Mims. The death of Moore, the first civil rights assassination in the United States, served as a symbol for Florida blacks who realized how far they still had to go to achieve equality.

The mid-1950s and early 1960s brought nationally noticed bus boycotts and lunch-counter sit-ins to Tallahassee, Daytona Beach, Jacksonville, and St. Augustine. In the late 1950s Florida Governor Leroy Collins, who started his career as a segregationist, spoke out in favor of the rights of blacks. In the late 1970s Governor Reubin Askew was the first Florida politician to put words into action and appointed many blacks to prominent positions throughout state government.

FLORIDA SITES

For general travel information contact the Florida Division of Tourism: 126 W. Van Buren St., Tallahassee, FL 32399. (904) 488-7300.

For information on the Florida Black Heritage Trail—a compilation of sites, buildings and points of interest regarding black history in Florida—contact the Florida Bureau of Historic Preservation: R.A. Gray Bldg., 500 South Bronough St., Tallahassee, FL 32399. (904) 487-2333. The bureau publishes a guidebook on the trail available to the public free of charge.

AMELIA ISLAND

American Beach—Located 37 miles north of Jacksonville on Amelia Island, off Hwy. A1A between Fernandina Beach and Amelia Island Plantation. Established in the 1920s, this 50-acre coastal property was purchased by blacks when other beaches in the area were off limits to blacks. Still a black beach, it is now being restored.

BUSHNELL

Dade Battlefield State Historic Site—off SR 476, west of Hwy. 301. Hours: grounds open Thurs.- Mon. 9-5. Site of the 1835 Dade Massacre, a bloody battle between Seminole Indians, who were aided by a group of escaped slaves, and Major Francis Dade and his troops. At the end of the battle, Dade and all but four of his men were dead. The Dade Massacre marked the beginning of the most costly of the country's Indian Wars.

CLEARWATER

Dorothy Thompson African-American Museum—1501 Madison Ave. North. (813) 447-1037. Hours: by appointment only. The museum houses a private collection of books by black authors, records, tapes, art and artifacts from the first 75 black families who settled in Clearwater.

COCOA

Harry T. Moore Center—307 Avocado Ave. Named in honor of the former president of Brevard County's NAACP, this single-story concrete structure built in 1924 served as the first black school in Cocoa. It is currently a childcare facility and community center.

Malissa Moore Home—215 Stone St. in the Richard E. Stone Historic District. Not open to the public. This private home, built in 1890, was originally located by the Indian River. It was later moved to its present location where it became a boarding house and occasionally hosted railroad entrepreneur Henry M. Flagler. Malissa Moore, an active Cocoa area black woman, helped establish the Mt. Moriah A.M.E. Church.

CORAL GABLES

MacFarlane Homestead Historic District—bounded by Oak Ave. on the north, Grand Ave. on the south, Brooker St. on the east, and Jefferson St. on the west. The residences in this district were built in the 1920s and 1930s as one-story frame bungalows and small "shot-gun" houses for blacks.

University of Miami, Black Heritage Museum—Dickinson Dr., Bldg. 37B. (305) 284-2855. Hours: Mon.-Fri., 9-5. A museum, library and gallery with a permanent collection of black heritage art including masks, paintings and carvings from South Africa, Ghana, Kenya, the Ivory Coast and Haiti.

CRESTVIEW

Carver-Hill Memorial Recreation Center/Museum—Fairview Park, 900 McClelland St. (904) 682-3494. Hours:

by appointment. A historical museum dedicated to the preservation of black culture, heritage, and contributions of blacks in Crestview.

DAYTONA BEACH

Bethune-Cookman College—640 Second Ave. (904) 255-1401. Founded in 1904 by black educator Mary McLeod Bethune for blacks. Bethune's home, a white frame house located on the campus, is open to the public. In addition, the college's Carl Swisher Library houses artifacts and materials on Bethune and Florida black history.

Howard Thurman House—614 Whitehall St. The childhood home of influential black theologian/educator Howard Thurman is located in one of the oldest residential sections of Daytona Beach. Thurman was the first black student in the area to receive an eighth grade diploma and pass the entrance examination for high school. This helped pave the way for educational equality in Florida's public school system.

Jackie Robinson Baseball Park—City Island. Named for baseball Hall of Famer Jackie Robinson who played his first major league game in Daytona Beach in 1946.

Museum of Arts and Sciences—1040 Museum Blvd. (904) 255-0285. Hours: Tues.-Fri. 9-4, Sat.-Sun. 12-5. Exhibits include a wing dedicated to the history of black Floridians and one of the best African art collections in the Southeast.

EATONVILLE

Eatonville—North of Orlando, between Winter Park and Maitland. Incorporated in 1887, Eatonville is the oldest, black municipality in the U.S. Birthplace (1901) of Zora Neale Hurston, author and black folklorist, it remains a predominantly black community today.

ELLENTON

J.P. Benjamin Memorial and Gamble Plantation— South of St. Petersburg on Hwy. 301. (813) 723-4536. Hours: Thurs.-Mon. 9:30-4:30. Once a 1,500 acre sugar plantation that employed 300 slaves. Now a memorial housed in a white frame mansion built in 1845.

FORT GEORGE ISLAND

Kingsley Plantation State Historic Site— 11676 Palmetto Ave. about 25 miles northeast of Jacksonville on the banks of the St. Johns River. (904) 251-3122. Hours: daily 8-5. A restored nineteenth-century cotton plantation once owned by slave trader Zephaniah Kingsley. Although Kingsley was married to an African woman, he believed that slavery was the only method of assuring the success of agriculture in the South. Tours of the plantation and remains of slave quarters are given about every two hours.

FORT LAUDERDALE

Museum of Archaeology— 203 S.W. First Ave. (305) 525-8778. Hours: Tues.-Sat. 10-4, Sun. 1-4. The Museum of Archaeology houses permanent displays on natural history featuring Tequesta Indians, geology, evolution, marine archaeology, and African tribal arts.

Museum of Art— 1 East Las Olas Blvd. (305) 525-5500. Hours: Tues. 11-9, Wed.-Sat. 10- 5. American and European art from the late nineteennth century to the present. A permanent collection featuring folk art paintings and sculptures of American Indians and West Africans.

Musicians Exchange Cafe— 729 W. Sunrise Blvd. (305) 764-1912. Hours: Open nightly except Wed.; hours vary. A cozy and crowded late-night club that hosts national jazz and blues acts.

Old Dillard High School—10001 N.W. 4th St. (305) 797-4800. Built in 1924, this is one of the oldest buildings in Fort Lauderdale, and was the first school for blacks in the area. It still serves as an educational and cultural center for the surrounding community.

FORT MYERS

Etta Powell Home—2764 Lime St. A private residence not open to the public, this home once hosted black major league baseball players who came to Fort Myers for spring training but were not allowed in the area's hotels.

Paul Lawrence Dunbar School—1857 Hight St. Constructed in 1927, the Dunbar School represented a landmark accomplishment when it opened as the first high school for blacks in the Dunbar community of Fort Myers. It remains a community school.

FORT PIERCE

Zora Neale Hurston House—1734 School Court St. The only known house still standing in which Hurston lived. She resided here while she was a reporter for *The Fort Pierce Chronicle*. The home is now a private residence.

GAINESVILLE

Florida Museum of Natural History—Museum Rd. University of Florida campus. (904) 392-1721. Hours: Tues.-Sat. 10-4, Sun. 1-4. Included in the museum's collection is the Fort Mose Exhibit, a diorama with replicas and archeological artifacts of the first free black community in the U.S.

Josiah Walls State Historical Marker—University Avenue between 1st and 2nd Sts. The marker commemorates the first black U.S. congressman elected from Florida.

Pleasant Street Historic District—Listed on the National Register of Historic Places, this is the oldest and largest continually inhabited black residential neighborhood in the Gainesville area. The district has served as the center for black commerce, education, entertainment, and religious life in the city.

JACKSONVILLE

Bethel Baptist Institutional Church—1058 Hogan St. Built in 1904, this Neo-classical Revival-style building has served as the focal point for the religious and community life of Jacksonville's black citizens.

Edward Waters College—1658 Kings Rd. (904) 355-3030. One of the many sites on Florida's Black Heritage Trail, Edward Waters College is the oldest of Jacksonville's four colleges. It was founded by the African Methodist Episcopal Church and was originally for former slaves. The college's Centennial Hall, built in 1916, was built by Rev. R.L. Brown, one of the few black architects and builders of the period. It now houses the college's library.

James Weldon Johnson Birthplace (1871). The first black to pass the Florida Bar Examinations, performer, diplomat, a leader in the NAACP, and author of *Autobiography of an Ex-Colored Man* and *God's Trombone*.

Masonic Temple Building—410 Broad St. This six-story brick structure, built in 1912 by the Black Masons of Florida, serves as the headquarters of the Masons of the State of Florida Grand East and focal point for the black community's fraternal activities.

"Mother" Midway A.M.E. Church—1456 Van Buren St.

(904) 356-9044. The first black independent church organization in Florida established in 1865. While the original church building has been replaced with a new one, the congregation has been in continuous existence since its founding and Sunday services are still held.

Robert Lee Hayes Birthplace (1942). Olympic champion, professional football player, and for a time,the "world's fastest human."

Stanton High School—521 W. Ahsley St. Stanton High School was the first public school built for black children in Jacksonville. The masonry structure, completed in 1917, is currently in need of restoration.

KEY WEST

Bahama Village - Duval and Petronia Sts. The Village is an integral part of the Old Town Historic District of Key West. This community of early Bahamian immigrants has maintained its island character.

LAKE BUENA VISTA

Walt Disney World EPCOT Center—(407) 824-4500. Hours: Sun-Fri. 9-9, Sat. 9a.m.-10p.m. EPCOT Center's World Showcase and American Pavilion of Future World both offer a taste of African and African-American history.

LAKE CITY

Florida Sports Hall of Fame—601 Hall of Fame Dr. off US 90, (904) 758-1310. Hours: Mon.-Sat. 9-p.m., Sun 10-7. Founded in 1958 by members of the Florida Sports Writers Association as a tribute to the great sports figures of Florida. Exhibits include career highlights of black athletes Althea Gibson, Bob Hayes, Larry Little and Andre Dawson, and Alonzo S. "Jake" Gaither.

MANDARIN

Mandarin—Small Florida town near Jacksonville where Harriet Beecher Stowe, author of *Uncle Tom's Cabin*, spent the winters of 1867-1884 and was active in the Florida movement for abolition.

MARATHON

Adderly House—5550 Overseas Hwy. This Bahamian-style house, built in 1906 by a black Bahamian immigrant, is the only documented historic site in the Florida Keys settled by blacks. It is a private residence not open to the public.

MELBOURNE

Cambell Park—Intersection of Melbourne Court and New Haven Ave. A triangular tree-lined point of land that was once owned by Peter Wright, one of the first black settlers of the 1800s.

MIAMI

Black Archives History and Research Foundation—Joseph Caleb Community Center, 5400 N.W. 22 Ave. (305) 638-6064. Hours: Mon.-Fri. 10-5. Educational exhibits and special programs devoted to the study of African-American history in southern Florida. Inquire about Black Heritage Trail tours in southern Florida.

Black Heritage Museum—3301 Coral Way. (305) 446-7304. Hours: Mon.-Fri. 11-4, Sat.-Sun. 1-4. A large exhibit of masks and artifacts primarily from the west coast of Africa.

Booker T. Washington High School—1200 N.W. 6th Ave. (305) 324-8900. Built in 1926, this was the first school in South Florida to provide a 12th grade education for black students.

Caribbean Marketplace—5927 N.E. 2 Ave. (305) 758-8708. Hours: Tues.- Thurs. 10:30-7, Fri.-Sat. 10:30-9, Sun. 10:30-5. Designed to resemble the Iron Market of Port-au-Prince, Haiti, the Marketplace is a colorful focal point of the neighborhood of Little Haiti. The open-air booths sell Caribbean art, crafts, clothing and food. Weekends usually bring live Caribbean music.

Coconut Grove—Charles Ave. Adjacent to the Coconut Grove Playhouse, Charles Ave. was where Miami's first black pioneers, mostly from the nearby Bahamas, settled. It was also the area of the Magic Knights of Dade Festival which was the 1915 forerunner of the Orange Bowl Festival. Many historic, Bahamian-style homes still line the street and at the western end of Charles Avenue is one of the oldest cemeteries in Miami.

It was in the Bahamian community of Miami that Oscar-wining actor Sydney Poitier was born. His father was a Bahamian tomato farmer. Poitier received the American Film Insititute's Life Achievement Award in 1992 and is most noted for his roles in *Lilies of the Field*, *In the Heat of the Night*, and *Guess Who's Coming to Dinner*. He was the first black film actor to leave his footprints in the famous cement of Mann's Chinese Theater in Hollywood.

Dorsey House—250 N.W. 9th St. Not open to the public. Constructed in 1913, this was the family home of black pioneer businessman Dana Albert Dorsey who helped establish South Florida's first black-owned bank and was a noted philanthropist.

Florida Memorial College—15800 N.W. 42 Ave. (305) 625-4141. A predominantly black Christian college dedicated to offering advanced educational opportunities for students at the lower end of the social and economic scale.

Historical Museum of Southern Florida—101 W. Flagler St. (305) 375-1492. Hours: Mon.-Sat. 10-5, Sun. 12-5. The museum collection includes a permanent display depicting early black settlers to Miami and their contributions to the city.

Lincoln Memorial Park Cemetery—N.W. 46th St and N.W. 30th Ave. Lincoln Memorial opened in 1924 and for decades served as the main cemetery for blacks in Miami. Black pioneers buried here include Dana Albert Dorser, Miami's first black millionaire, and the first black woman to serve in the Florida Legislature, Gwen Sawer Cherry.

Lyric Theater—N.W. 2nd Ave. and 9th St. Opened in 1919 by prominent black businessman Geda Walker, the Lyric was once one of the most beautiful black playhouses in the South. It was here, in the 1930s and 40s, that Count Bassie, Billie Holiday and Cab Calloway played their last sets after performing in Miami Beach. The theater was converted to a church in 1960, and is currently being restored to a theater again.

Martin Luther King, Jr., Parade & Festival—(305) 261-8383. An annual celebration of the birthday and accomplishments of Martin Luther King, Jr., usually held in January at varied locations.

McCrory's Department Store—23 E. Flagler St. (305) 371-1361. Hours: Mon.-Sat. 9 -7, Sun. 10-5. One of the oldest buildings in Miami dating back to 1906. This is where Miami blacks staged a historic lunch-counter sit-in at the store's cafeteria during the civil rights movement of the 1960s.

Miami-Bahamas Goombay Festival—Grand Ave. Coconut Grove. (305) 445-8292. An annual June street party that has become one of the largest black heritage festivals in the U.S. Goombay festivities date back to the freeing of the slaves in the Bahamas, and today celebrates Miami's Bahamian culture.

Miami Times—900 N.W. 54 St. (305) 757-1147. Established in 1923 by Bahamian native Henry S.E. Reeves, the *Miami Times* is the largest black newspaper in South Florida. By appointment only; call ahead for an informal tour.

Overtown Square—N.W. 2 Ave. between 6th and 10th Sts. Once the center of Miami's black community formerly called Avenue G or the "Great Black Way." The neighborhood's Mary Elizabeth Hotel, now torn down, hosted great blacks such as Supreme Court Justice Thurgood Marshall and Adam Clayton Powell.

Studio One-83—2860 N.W. 183 St. (305) 621-7295. Hours: Thurs.-Sun. 8 p.m. (closing times vary). A 2,500-seat concert hall and dance club that features R & B, jazz and Caribbean music.

Sunshine Jazz Organization —Promoter of Miami area jazz and blues concerts. Jazz hotline: (305) 382-3938. Blues hotline: (305) 666-6656.

Sunstreet Festival—(305) 638-4709. An annual celebration of Miami's African-American culture usually held in November at varied locations.

Tobacco Road—626 S. Miami Ave. (305) 374-1198. Hours: daily 11:30 a.m.-4 a.m. Holder of the oldest liquor license in Miami, the Road is a first-rate blues joint that hosts national R & B acts amid a funky decor of Miami memorabilia.

Visitor's Guide to Black Miami—(305) 751-8648. Published by the Miami-Dade Chamber of Commerce, this annual guide highlights Miami's black heritage, communities and businesses.

MILTON

Mount Pilgram African Baptist Church—Corner of Alice and Clara Sts. One block west of Canal St. near the Milton Historic District. Constructed in 1916, this Gothic Revival brick church was designed by Wallace A. Rayfiled, a leading black architect in the South during the early twentieth century.

MIMS

Mims—This small, east coast town north of Titusville was where white racists in 1951 bombed the home of Harry T. Moore, head of Florida's NAACP, killing Moore and his wife. The incident cemented the efforts of Florida blacks to fight for equality.

OCALA

Doe Lake Park—Off SR 314-A between Rds. 40 and 42 in the Ocala National Forest. Doe Lake was designed and established by the U.S. Forest Service as a recreational area for blacks.

OLUSTEE

Olustee Battlefield Historic Memorial— 2 1/2 miles east of Olustee on U.S. 90 about 50 miles west of Jacksonville, (904) 752-3866. Hours: Mon.-Thurs. 8-5. Site of the largest Civil War battle on Florida soil where the 8th U.S. Colored Troops fought in February 1864. Features a short walking tour, small interpretive museum, and a 1869 Curtis & Allison lithograph of the 8th U.S. Colored Troops.

OPA-LOCKA

Opa-Locka City Hall—777 Sharazad Blvd. (305) 688-4611. Hours: Mon.-Fri. 9-5. Located northwest of Miami, Opa-Locka is a predominantly black city. Its City Hall and nineteen other buildings in the surrounding area, are listed on the National Register of Historic Places and are noted for their unique Moorish architecture inspired by the *Tales from the Arabian Nights*.

ORANGE SPRINGS

Orange Springs Community Church—About 25 miles northeast of Ocala on Hwy. 315. (no phone) A simple but impressive country structure built in 1818, this church served both blacks and whites. It has an upstairs "slave balcony" and an easy-open back door that allowed early settlers to flee quickly from Indian raids. The nearby cemetery is full of Civil War gravestones, and services are still held each Sunday.

ORLANDO

Callahan Neighborhood—Located between Colonial Dr. to the north, Central Ave. to the east, Division St. to the south, and Orange Blossom Trail to the west. This neighborhood, started in 1886, is one of the oldest continuing black communities in Orlando. It includes the Callahan Neighborhood Center, founded in 1895, one of the oldest educational facilities for blacks in Orlando.

J.A. Colyer Building—27-29 Church St. Currently an Irish pub, this Romanesque-style building was built in 1911 by J.A. Colyer and served as his tailor shop. It was one of the first black-owned businesses located in the white business district of downtown Orlando.

Orlando Museum of Art—2416 North Mills Ave. (407) 896-4231. Hours: Tues.- Thurs. 9-5, Fri. 9-7:30, Sat. 10 -5,

Sun. 12-5. One of the first museums in the U.S. to receive professional accreditation by the American Association of Museums, the Orlando Museum of Art hosts a permanent collection of twentieth-century American and African art.

PENSACOLA

Julee Cottage—210 East Zaragoza St. (904) 444-8905. Hours: Mon.-Sat. 10a.m.-4p.m. Located in the Historic Pensacola Village, this historic cottage, built in the early 1800s, was the home of a free black woman named Julee Penton. It now contains an exhibit on the history of blacks in west Florida.

Saint Michael's Creole Benevolent Association Hall—416 E. Government St. in the Seville Square Historic District. (904) 444-8908. Hours: Mon.-Sat. 10-4:30. Built in 1896, this hall was used to accommodate the cultural activities of the city's racially mixed Creoles who were isolated from both the white and black communities of the city.

ST. AUGUSTINE

Butler Beach Park—on Anastasia Island, about 8 miles south of the city on Hwy. A1A. Originally developed and named for black businessman Frank Bertran Butler, an important figure in Jacksonville's Lincolnville area. In 1963, the land was donated by Butler and turned into a resort area and recreational park for blacks.

Castillo de San Marcos—One Castillo Dr. (904) 829-6506. Hours: daily 9a.m.-5:15p.m. Located in downtown St. Augustine, the national monument at this fort, constructed in the late 1600s, contains an exhibit on black history and the role of free blacks in Spanish Florida.

Fort Mose—An island outpost of St. Augustine 2 1/2

miles north of the city off US 1, accessible only by boat; for entry information contact the Florida State Parks Service at (904) 461-2030. Fort Mose, established in 1738, was the first free black community in the U.S.

Lincolnville—Martin Luther King,Jr., Ave. in the south quadrant of St. Augustine. Lincolnville is an historic black neighborhood of the city dating back to the 1800s with several historic homes and commercial buildings still standing. It has the greatest concentration of late nineteenth-century architecture in St. Augustine.

Mission Nombre de Dios—27 Ocean Ave. (904) 824-3045. Hours: daily 9 a.m. - 5 p.m. Site where, on September 8, 1565, Pedro Menendez de Aviles landed with a band of white settlers and black slaves who founded St. Augustine. The event is depicted in a diorama at this site.

SANFORD

John M. Hurston House—621 E. 6th St. Not open to the public. Historic home of John Hurston, father of noted author and anthropologist Zora Neale Hurston, who lived here in the early 1900s.

St. James A.M.E. Church—819 Cypress Ave. This red brick, English Gothic Revival-style structure built in 1913 is an excellent example of the work of black architect Prince W. Spears.

SARASOTA

Historical Marker—Central Ave. and 6th St. Honoring the first black community of Sarasota established in the late 1800s along 6th Street. Dozens of black-owned businesses and homes still stand.

SUMATRA

Fort Gadsden Historic Memorial— 6 miles southwest of Sumatra on SR 65. (904) 670-8988. Hours: daily 8a.m.-sunset. The historic marker on this site explains that it was once an abandoned British fort that was taken over by Indians and runaway slaves and renamed Fort Negro.

TALLAHASSEE

C.K. Steele Memorial—111 W. Tennessee St. A statue and marker that commemorates the work of Rev. Charles Kenzie Steele, one of Florida's noted civil rights leaders.

Florida Agricultural & Mechanical University, Martin Luther King, Jr., Blvd. (904) 599-3000. A state university of Florida established in 1887 for blacks. Site of the **Black Archives Research Center and Museum**, (904) 599-3020. Hours: Mon.-Fri. 9-4. Housed in one of Tallahassee's oldest buildings, the museum contains artifacts, books and exhibits on black culture and history.

Gibbs Cottage—South Adams St. Constructed in 1894, Gibbs Cottage was once the home of Thomas Van Renssalaer Gibbs, a member of the Florida Legislature who, in 1887, introduced a bill which resulted in the founding of the Florida Normal and Industrial School for Negroes, now Florida A & M University.

John G. Riley House—419 East Jefferson St., (904) 224-0697. Hours: Mon., Wed., Fri. 10a.m.-1p.m. Home of John G. Riley, principal of the first local high school for blacks. Now houses the local chapter of the NAACP.

Old City Cemetery—Martin Luther King, Jr., Blvd. and Park Ave. (904) 574-5320. Hours: daily 8-7. Pioneers and their slaves are buried here, along with black and white confederate and federal troops from the 1865 Battle of Natural Bridge.

TAMPA

Busch Gardens—3000 East Busch Blvd. (813) 971-8282. Hours: daily 9:30- 6. A 300-acre turn-of-the-century African-theme park with one of the largest collections of African animals in the U.S.

Museum of African-American Art—1308 Marion St. (813) 272-2466. Hours: Tues.-Sat. 10-4:30, Sun. 1-4:30. One of the oldest collections of African-American art in the U.S. dating back to the 1800s.

Museum of Science and Industry, 4801 E. Fowler Ave. (813) 985-5531. Hours: Sun.-Thurs. 9-4:30., Fri.-Sat. 9-9. The museum collection includes the permanent exhibit Black Contributors to Science and Inventions.

TITUSVILLE

Spaceport U.S.A.—on FL 405, 11 miles east of I-95. (407) 452-2121. Hours: daily 9a.m.-sunset. Included in the Space Center's exhibits is information on black astronauts Dr. Ronald McNair and Lt. Col. Guion Bluford, Jr.

WEST PALM BEACH

Northwest Neighborhood Historic District—The northwest section of downtown West Palm Beach. In the late 1890s, the black residents of the so called "Styx" section of the city were forced to move to this Northwest section. The district is the only remaining portion of the original black settlement, and includes the Tabernacle Missionary Baptist Church, which served as the first public school for blacks in Palm Beach County.

WOODVILLE

Natural Bridge Battlefield State Historic Site— Ochlockonee River State Park, US Hwy. 319, (904) 962-2771. Hours: daily 9 a.m.-5p.m. Site where the 22nd and 99th U.S. Colored Infantry Regiments and others sought to capture St. Marks and Tallahassee in the 1865 Battle of Natural Bridge.

SOUTH CAROLINA

South Carolina's location and topography determined the lifeways of its slave inhabitants. Its watery rice plantations, cleared, diked, and farmed by slaves who had been rice cultivators in Africa, supported the South's richest aristocracy.

Unlike the family farm economy of a colony like Virginia, South Carolina was home to large-scale commercial plantations, resulting in a constant need for more and more slaves. Native Americans were pressed into slavery in great numbers in South Carolina; by 1710 slaves had become the majority population of the colony, numbering 5,500, almost a third of them Indians. Wars and disease nearly annihilated the Indian population, and from 1720 on Africans constituted the vast majority of slaves.

Along the Atlantic coast near Charleston, South Carolina, is a string of low, flat islands known as the South Carolina sea islands. During slavery, these hitherto uninhabited islands, among them Johns, James, Wadamalow, and Foley, offered refuge to escaped slaves, who were joined after the Civil War by members of the First South Carolina Volunteers, a black regiment, who rowed their way across the bays and took land on the islands for their own.

For generations, the inhabitants of these islands lived

relatively undisturbed. Called "Geechee," their Gullah dialect, a combination of West African and West Indian with English, is the only fairly "pure" form of pidginized English spoken in the United States today.

Robert Smalls was a Gullah. Born into slavery in 1839, he was pressed into service for the Confederacy as a crewman on the *Planter*, a transport steamer used to haul guns. On the night of May 13, 1863, while the white captain and crew were ashore, Smalls and other black crewmen sailed the ship out of Charleston harbor and surrendered it to the Union navy. After the *Planter's* Union captain deserted under enemy fire, Smalls was given command. During the Reconstruction period following the war, Smalls served first as state legislator and then as congressman from South Carolina.

Robert Brown Elliott was another Reconstructionist Era black state legislator and later congressman from South Carolina. Born in the North, he moved to South Carolina looking for opportunity in 1867, drawn by the state's special demographics. Of the eleven ex-Confederate states, in only two, South Carolina and Mississippi, did newly enfranchised blacks constitute a majority of the voting population and hold undisputed control of their state legislatures.

On the sea island of St. Helena, the Penn School, one of the first schools for black adults, was established in 1862 by two Pennsylvania Quakers. Mary McLeod Bethune, the noted black educator, was born in Mayesville.

Charleston resonates with black history, with its Old Slave Market and its tradition of slave revolts. In Charleston County, in the vicinity of Rantowles, the most serious slave insurrection of the colonial period occurred at the Stono River. The Denmark Vesey House, declared a National Historic Landmark in 1976, is at 56 Bull Street in Charleston. Also in Charleston is Catfish Row, the strip of tenements that was the setting for the Gershwin opera *Porgy and Bess.*

South Carolina is also important to more recent African-American history; Jesse Jackson was born in Greenville in 1941.

SOUTH CAROLINA SITES

For general travel information contact the South Carolina Division of Tourism, P.O. Box 71, Columbia, S.C. 29202. (803) 734-0235.

ATLANTIC BEACH

Atlantic Beach—Better known as "Black Pearl," this strip of Atlantic coast in Horry County and other surrounding properties are owned predominantly by blacks. For the first time in 1992, and Afro-Fest was held during Labor Day weekend in Atlantic Beach.

BEAUFORT

Gullah Festival—P.O.B. 83, Beaufort, SC 29901. (803) 525-0628. An annual cultural festival held in late May that highlights the fine arts, customs, dress, language and culture of the Gullah people, African-Americans who live in the coastal districts and sea islands of South Carolina , Georgia and northeastern Florida.

Robert Smalls Monument—Baptist Tabernacle Church, 907 Craven St. (803) 524-0376. Robert Smalls was a congressman, Civil War hero and member of the Gullah people of the lowlands of South Carolina. Born into slavery in 1839, Smalls was an expert at handling sailboats and steamers. While working as a crewman on the *Planter*, a Confederate transport steamer used to haul guns and ammunition, the 23-year-old Smalls along with other black crewmembers plotted their escape to freedom. In May of 1862 Smalls and his fellow slaves waited for the white captain and crew to go ashore, and in the darkness of night sailed the Confederate ship into Union hands. Once a free man, Smalls joined the Northern fleet and when the Union captain of the *Planter* deserted under enemy attack, Smalls was given the ship's command. After the war, he became a Gullah statesman and, in 1875, a congressman. His former home at 511 Prince Street in Beaufort is listed on the National Register of Historic Places, but is not open to the public.

CHARLESTON

African-American Spiritual Concert—Organized by the Drayton Hall Visitors Services, 3380 Ashley River Rd., Charleston 29414. (803) 766-0188. An annual event held after Christmas in historic Drayton Hall, this concert presents the dramatic, musical communication that emerged during slavery. Spirituals, many in the Gullah language, are performed by the Senior Lights, a popular and inspiring choir from Johns Island near Charleston.

Avery Research Center for African-American History and Culture—College of Charleston, 67 George St. (803) 792-5741. Hours: Mon.-Fri. 10-1 and 2-4:30. The center is a repository for African-American history and culture, including extensive materials on the Gullah culture of the sea islands. Lectures, workshops and exhibits are offered.

Boone Hall Plantation—Eight miles north of Charleston on US 17. (803) 884-4371. Mon.-Sat. 8:30-6:30, Sun. 1-5p.m., April 1 - Labor Day; Mon.-Sat. 9-5, Sun. 1-4 the rest of the year. One of the largest pre-Civil War cotton plantations in the South, Boone Hall was developed in

1676 and once encompassed 17,000 acres and employed more than 1,000 slaves. The magnificent manor house, gin house, smokehouse, slave quarters and garden walls were all produced by slave labor. Several original slave cabins still stand in what is called the only remaining "slave street" in the southeast. Boone Hall is still a working farm.

Cabbage Row—89-91 Church St. This row of tenement houses got its name from the home-grown cabbages that black residents sold from their windows. It was used as a literary model for Catfish Row in the book *Porgy* by Dubose Heyward which went on to become the Broadway play *Porgy and Bess*. Not far away from Church Street is St. Michael's Alley, noted for the vendors who sell handwoven sweetgrass baskets. The authentic art of weaving these baskets can be traced back to the West African tradition brought over during the early days of slavery.

Charleston Museum—360 Meeting St. (803) 722-2996. Mon.-Sat. 9-5, Sun. 1-5. Considered one of the oldest museums in the country, the Charleston Museum was established in 1773 and specializes in exhibits on Charleston and the South Carolina low country. It also has displays on slavery, African-American crafts, archeology, natural history, and a special room for children.

Denmark Vesey House—56 Bull St. A National Historic Landmark not open to the public. This modest house was the home of Denmark Vesey, a free black carpenter who was instrumental in plotting of an 1822 slave revolt in Charleston. When an informant squealed on the plan, 36 people were executed.

Drayton Hall—3380 Ashley River Rd. (803) 766-0188. Hours: daily 10-5 March-Oct., 10-3 the rest of the year.

An immense, two-story brick house built in 1738 by John Drayton, a member of His Majesty's council. This was the only Ashley River home not vandalized by the Union troops invasion of 1865. Jointly owned by the National Trust for Historic Preservation and the State of South Carolina, this landmark is in its original condition and is considered the finest example of Georgian Palladian architecture in the nation.

Emannuel African Methodist Episcopal Church—110 Calhoun St. (803) 722-2561. One of the oldest A.M.E. congregations in the South, this is the latest of several churches to house the congregation which was founded in 1791. In 1822, the congregation's church was closed when authorities learned that Denmark Vesey, a free black, used the sanctuary while making plans for a slave insurrection.

Middlton Place —Northwest of Charleston on SC 61, fourteen miles from the junction with US 17. (803) 556-6020. Hours: daily 9-5. Although much of this historic plantation home was destroyed during the Civil War, there are several restored buildings still standing. When built, over 100 slaves labored on the project for ten years. The property contains the oldest landscaped gardens in America, and offers demonstrations of spinning, weaving, blacksmithing, candle-making, carpentry, and pottery making. House tours show visitors the internal workings of an eighteenth-century plantation.

Mojo Arts Festival—Sponsored by the Charleston Office of Cultural Affairs, 133 Church St. (803) 724-7309. An annual festival that runs from late September through the beginning of October, this ten-day celebration of the African-American and Caribbean cultures found in the low country of South Carolina offers lectures, art exhibits, stage performances, and jazz concerts.

Slave Auction Building—6 Chalmers St. Since the city of Charleston disallowed the sale of slaves on the street, this building, formerly called Ryan's Mart, served as the main trading market for the city's slave auctions. A similar building at the corner of State and Assembly Streets served the same function.

COLUMBIA

Annual Jubilee Festival—(803) 252-1450. An annual event held the last Saturday in September, this celebration features African-American music, dance and crafts.

First Baptist Church—1306 Hampton St. (803) 256-4251. This church, built in 1859, was the site of the opening of the first Secession Convention in December 1860 which led to the vote for the state's withdrawal from the Union, one of the events that led to the start of the Civil War. The church's original slave gallery has been preserved.

Mann-Simons Cottage/Museum of African-American Culture—1403 Richland St. (803) 252-1450. Hours: Tues.-Sat 10:15-3:15. Celia Mann was a slave who bought her freedom in Charleston, then walked 180 miles to Columbia, where she purchased this property. The midwife/seamstress had four daughters, one of whom married Simons. The house, built in 1850, stayed in the family for a century. Though it was slated for demolition, the local historical association bought it and turned it into a museum that includes family portraits, period antiques, African art and exhibits, and a gift shop.

McKissick Museum—University of South Carolina campus, two blocks south of the State House near the intersection of Bull and Pendelton Sts. (803) 777-7251. Hours: Mon.-Fri. 9-4, Sat. 10-5, Sun. 1-5. Permanent and rotating exhibits that focus on Southern and black folk art, culture, and history.

Ones United—(803) 765-2300 or 787-8199. Hours: Mon.-Fri. 9-5. A tour operator that specializes in historical and present-day tours of sites in the greater Columbia area which have importance to African-Americans. Inspirational youth tours are also offered.

Randolph Cemetery—Elmwood Ave. Extension. (803) 771-6417. Named for Benjamin Franklin Randolph, a black man elected as state senator in 1868, then shot and hanged during his campaign for re-election. Many prominent Columbia blacks are buried here.

South Carolina State Museum—301 Gervais St. (803) 737-4595. Hours: Mon.-Sat. 10-5, Sun. 1-5. In addition to a large, permanent exhibit on the history of South Carolina, the museum houses Antebellum Society, a permanent exhibit which includes displays on slavery, and black mourning and funeral customs. It also features rotating exhibits on African-American culture and history throughout the year.

DAUFUSKIE ISLAND

Daufuskie Island—Once a small rural island inhabited mainly by the descendants of former slaves and accessible only by boat. Pat Conroy wrote about Daufuskie in his novel *The Water Is Wide*, which was subsequently made into the movie *Conrack*. Several marinas on nearby Hilton Head Island offer scheduled tours. Parts of the island are now under resort development.

DENMARK

Voorhees College—Voorhees Rd. (803) 793-3351. This

predominantly black school of 550 students was founded in 1897 as an industrial training facility for blacks by Elizabeth Evan Wright, a protegé of Booker T. Washington.

FLORENCE

Florence Museum of Art—Graham and Spruce Sts. (803) 662-3351. Hours: Tues.-Sat. 10-5, Sun. 2-5 p.m. Closed in August. Along with a display on the history of South Carolina, this museum contains a collection of African art.

GEORGETOWN

Committee of African-American Observances—315 Gilbert St. (803) 546-6901. Hours: Mon.-Fri. 9-5. Dramas and ensembles from Africa and around the world are performed year-round at this center.

GREENVILLE

Greenville County Museum of Art—420 College St. (803) 271-7570. Hours: Tues.-Sat. 10-5, Sun. 1-5. Works by black artist Romare Bearden are included in this museum's modern American collection.

Greenville Cultural Exchange Center—700 Arlington Ave. (803) 232-9162. Hours: Tues.-Sun. 10-5. A black history resource center dedicated to the preservation of the black history and culture of Greenville. Included in the center is the Jesse Jackson Hall of Fame; Jackson is a native of Greenville.

Phyllis Wheatley Center—335 Greenacre Rd. (803) 235-3411. Hours: Mon.-Fri. 9-5. This community center was established in 1919 to provide educational and recreational outlets for blacks; it now provides services for all ethnic groups.

River Place Festival—An annual celebration held in early May, this festival brings well-known Motown artists to the banks of the Reedy River in Greenville to top off a spring weekend of arts and crafts and ethnic foods.

KINGSTREE

Williamsburg County Black Heritage Festival—(803) 354-9106. An annual folk festival held in late July that highlights traditional music and dance, arts and crafts, plus homemade ice cream and foods.

LANCASTER

Carolina Legends: A Musical Celebration—Lancaster County Council of the Arts, P.O. Box 613, Lancaster 29721. (803) 285-7451. A yearly outdoor festival held in early October at Andrew Jackson State Park, this celebration strives to showcase jazz greats who have connections with South Carolina.

MAYESVILLE

Mayesville—With its elegant old homes, Mayesville is the birthplace of Mary McLeod Bethune, educator and founder of Florida's Bethune-Cookman College. Born in 1875 of slave parents, she became special adviser to President Franklin D. Roosevelt and observer for the United States at the 1945 founding of the United Nations in San Francisco. She was also a prominent leader in the civil rights movement until her death.

MORRIS ISLAND

Morris Island—Near Charleston, Morris Island, with its massive fortress of Fort Wagner, controlled every sea approach to Charleston during the Civil War. In July 1863, the all-black 54th Massachusetts, under Colonel

Robert Gould Shaw, led the assault on Fort Wagner. Despite being caught in a deadly cross-fire, the men of the 54th stormed the walls of the fort, fighting with bayonets and clubbed rifles against artillery, rifle fire and grenades. Of the 650 black troops who fought that day, 272 lost their lives. Colonel Shaw was one of those killed and was buried with his men at Fort Wagner. Sergeant William Carney, although wounded several times, saved the regimental flag and was awarded the Medal of Honor for his bravery that day. The actual battle site of Fort Wagner no longer exists.

ORANGEBURG

I.P. Stanback Museum—South Carolina State College, 300 College St. (803) 5360-7174. Hours: Mon.-Fri. 9-4:30. Closed in summer. This modern museum focuses on history, science, and the fine arts. Its permanent collection includes the work of African-American artists William Johnson, Elton Fox, Romare Bearden, Jacob Lawrence, along with a substantial collection of art from Benin and Cameroon. An historic photo collection documents black life and history from the 1800s and early 1900s.

ROCK HILL

Africa Alive—Organized by the Museum of York County, 4621 Mt. Gallant Rd. (803) 329-2121. Africa Alive is an annual festival held in mid-February in conjunction with Black History Month that traces the traditions, customs and culture of Africans.

Museum of York County—4621 Mt. Gallant Rd. (803) 329-2121. Hours: Tues.-Sat. 10-5, Sun. 1-5. Along with a planetarium and nature trails, this museum holds a collection of mounted African animals, and arts and crafts from Africa in its Stans Africa Hall.

ST. HELENA ISLAND

Heritage Celebration—P.O. Box 126, St. Helena Island 29920. (803) 838-2432. An annual celebration held in early November, this festival pays tribute to sea island history and culture. It is held at the Penn School Historic District and Museum and includes arts and crafts exhibits, traditional spirituals, a fish fry and oyster roast.

Penn School Historic District and Museum—Land's End Rd. at Frogmore, a short drive from Beaufort on US 21. (803) 838-2432. After Federal troops gained control of St. Helena's Island in 1861, they confiscated plantation properties along with 10,000 slaves who were considered "contraband of war." Soon after, in the midst of the Civil War, missionaries and teachers arrived to offer schooling for the ex-slaves and formed the first school for freed slaves in the South. By the late 1800s, Penn offered classes in agriculture, homemaking and industrial arts. The school is currently the Penn Community Services Center and is listed on the National Register of Historic Places. It now serves as a bi-racial conference center while also offering classes for black residents of St. Helena.

York W. Bailey Museum—Located at Frogmore in the Penn Center Historical District. (803) 838-2432. Hours: daily 9-5. A museum dedicated to the heritage of blacks from the sea islands with exhibits on folk art, oral histories, photographs and antique tools. The museum also provides community services to the people of the area.

SHELDON

Oyotunji African Village—US 17-21, 50 miles south of Charleston, 45 miles north of Savannah. (803) 846-8900. Hours: daily 9-5 in the fall/winter, 9-8 in the spring/summer. A Yoruba-style African village run by volunteers who live on the property full-time. The village includes a palace inhabited by a king and his many wives, a museum that displays arts and crafts from Yoruba and Benin, a temple that explains the ancient gods and goddesses of southwestern Nigeria, and bazaar-style gift shops. Yoruba music and dance shows are featured regularly. Lodging is available with advance reservations.

SULLIVAN'S ISLAND

Sullivan's Island —Across the channel from Fort Sumter via US 17 and SC 703. Similar to Ellis Island in New York City, Sullivan's Island was where most of the plantation-bound slaves who arrived in America during the early 1800s first landed.

Fort Sumter National Monument—1214 Middle St. (803) 883-3123. Hours: daily from 9-5. Fort Sumter may be reached by tour boats from Charleston City Marina on Lockwood Boulevard in Charleston, and from Patriots Point Naval Museum in Mount Pleasant. Tours of the fort are conducted by the National Parks Service and there is a museum with artifacts from the war. It was under the guns of nearby Fort Sumter that black pilot Robert Smalls captured the Confederate ship *Planter* and piloted her out of the Charleston harbor. Fort Sumter, where the first shot of the Civil War was fired, is now a National Monument.

Old Slave Mart Library—Previously located in Charleston at the Old Slave Mart Museum, the library is now on Sullivan's Island, but is in the process of recovering from damages due to Hurricane Hugo, (803) 883-3797. Hours: By appointment only. The library houses over 20,000 books, pamphlets, historic documents, maps, engravings, prints, letters, and audio-visual materials relating to African-Americans and Africans.

NORTH CAROLINA

North Carolina's early history is closely tied to the first attempts at English colonialization of the New World; Roanoke Island was the site of the famous Lost Colony whose inhabitants vanished sometime after they landed in 1587. One of the original thirteen colonies, North Carolina depended for its growth on slaves who in early years produced tar, pitch, rosin, and turpentine and later provided the manpower for the labor-intensive crops of rice, indigo, tobacco, and cotton. In 1790 slaves numbered more than 100,000, approximately one-third of the total population.

While South Carolina's strident pro-slavery voices led the South into secession, North Carolina was a reluctant secessionist, seeking compromise to the last moment. Once it had thrown its lot in with the Confederacy, however, North Carolina fought with determination and after defeat experienced the same political and economic disruption.

Dred Wimberly was among the former slaves who held political office in North Carolina during Reconstruction. He served as a state representative in 1879 and a state senator in 1889 and is honored with a marker at Rocky Mount. Rocky Mount is also renowned as the "Capital of Gospel Singers."

Until 1970, North Carolina, with thirteen predominantly black colleges, had more institutions of higher learning for blacks than any other state. Among these was Palmer Institute, founded in Sedalia, North Carolina, in 1902 by Charlotte Hawkins Brown. A notable black woman for her time, Brown held honorary degrees from Wellesly College and Brown University and was the first black member of the national board of the YWCA. She traveled to Europe long before most blacks did and wrote a book on etiquette entitled *The Correct Thing*. Nat King Cole's widow, Maria, born Marie Hawkins, was raised by Dr. Brown, who did not approve of Maria's marriage to Cole but provided Maria's wedding gown. The marker on Burlington Road in Sedalia honoring Dr. Brown was North Carolina's first state historic site honoring an African-American.

Another notable African-American institution of higher learning is North Carolina Agricultural and Technical State University, founded in 1890 as an extension of Shaw University. There, on February 1, 1960, several black students began a spontaneous campaign of sit-ins at the local Woolworth's lunch counter. The movement spread like wildfire, and by February 10 students in five other Southern cities were conducting similar sit-ins. The student sit-in movement led directly to the founding in April of the Student Nonviolent Coordinating Committee (SNCC).

Creswell, North Carolina, is the site of Somerset Place, a plantation made famous through the efforts of Dorothy Redford. Inspired by Alex Haley's *Roots*, Redford went on a quest for her ancestors and those of the Collins family, who owned Somerset Place. Redford's research led in 1986 to one of the largest black family reunions ever held, and she is the guiding spirit behind its development.

NORTH CAROLINA SITES

For general travel information contact the North Carolina Travel and Tourism Division, 430 North Salisbury St., Raleigh, NC, 27611. (800) 847-4862.

ASHEVILLE

Biltmore Estate/Young Men's Institute—Three blocks north of I-50, off exit 40. (704) 255-1776. Hours: daily 9-5. This French Renaissance-style chateau with 35 acres of formal gardens was built as a private residence for the George Vanderbilt family in the late 1800s. As an act of gratitude to the many black craftsmen who labored on the elaborate mansion, Vanderbilt built an 18,000 square foot, three-story recreation center in 1892, currently known as the **Young Men's Institute**, at the Culture Center, 39 South Market St. Hours: daily 9-5. (704) 252-4614. In 1896, Vanderbilt sold the property for $10,000 to a group of black Asheville businessmen who established the Young Men's Institute to offer vocational education to young blacks. The center sponsors youth programs and monthly exhibits featuring black artists.

CAPE HATTERAS

Cape Hatteras National Seashore—Known as the Outer Banks by Carolinians. In 1895 Captain Richard Etheridge of the Pea Island Lifesaving Station, born a slave in 1842, began a rescue attempt that earned him and his black lifesaving crew a place in history. They rescued the crew and passengers of the *E.S. Newman,* lost in heavy seas and blown by a storm onto the rocks; the schooner's masts were stripped of their sails by the wind. Etheridge was the first black commander of the station, which was established in 1880, and his bravery is still remembered by the present-day Coast Guard. The station continued as the only all-black lifesaving station in the country until closing in 1952. All signs of the station have been swept away, but for a simple marker.

CHARLOTTE

Afro-American Cultural Center—401 North Myers St. (704) 374-1565. Hours: Tues.-Sat. 10-6, Sun. 1-5. The mission of this center is to promote and preserve African-American culture through sponsoring emerging and established artists for various shows including music, dance, theater and visual arts.

McDonald's Cafeteria—2812 Beatties Ford Rd. (704) 393-8110. Hours: Mon.-Thurs. 7a.m.-11p.m., Fri.-Sat 7a.m.-12a.m., Sun. 7a.m.-8p.m. A well-known, black-owned restaurant that specializes in home-style Southern cooking: fried chicken, barbecue ribs, homemade cornbread. The owner, John W. McDonald, originally opened his McDonald's restaurant in New York City in 1955, and later moved it to Charlotte in 1969.

Spirit Square—345 N. College St. (704) 372-9664. An arts center in downtown Charlotte, this has three theaters that offer numerous dramatic and musical productions including jazz and special programs for African-Americans.

CRESWELL

Somerset Place—On Lake Phelps, nine miles south of Creswell via US 64 and minor roads. (919) 797-4560. Hours: Mon.-Sat. 9-5, Sun. 1-5. A nineteenth-century plantation established by Josiah Collins in 1785 built by several hundred slaves. Originally a vast swampland, this property was cleared by hand in order to plant rice fields. Many of the slaves used to work the land died of illness and exhaustion, but historians say that the Somerset Place slaves were better treated than most others in the area. When it was a working plantation, Somerset provided medical care, ministry services and comfortable living quarters for its slaves. When the Civil War hit, Somerset Place was all but destroyed and in the 1950s a restoration project brought parts of it back to life. Today, the remains of slave buildings, a hospital, chapel and the overseer's house can be seen. Tours of the mansion and surrounding buildings offer a glimpse of what nineteenth-century plantation life was like for both the master and the slaves.

DURHAM

NCCU Art Museum—Located on the North Carolina Central University campus. (919) 560-6211. Hours: Tues.-Fri. 9-5, Sun. 2-5. A portion of this museum focuses on African-American works of art including paintings, sculpture and graphics.

North Carolina Mutual Life Insurance Company—501 Willard St. (919) 682-9201. Housed in a building that is a National Historical Landmark, the North Carolina Mutual Life Insurance Company was founded by area blacks in 1898 during the days of Jim Crow. Today, it is one of the largest black-owned and operated businesses in the U.S. In addition to the NCMLI company, the town of Durham has many other successful black-owned businesses.

Stagville Center—Old Oxford Hwy., seven miles northeast of the NC 1004 and NC 501 intersection. (919) 620-0120. Hours: Mon.-Fri. 9-4. Originally a plantation of several thousand acres, Stagville was the focal point of an enormous estate owned by the Bennehan-Cameron family. In its prime during the late 1800s, it utilized 900 slaves to run the property. In addition to tending the fields and working in the great house, many of the slaves were trained artisans and craftsmen. Several slave communities once existed on the estate including the Horton Grove quarters which housed about 100 slaves in small, two-story cabins. After completing their plantation-related chores, the slaves of Stagville community tended to their own vegetable gardens, maintained their cabins, hunted, fished, and conducted community affairs. Many years ago, scholars found a walking cane that had been hidden away in the main house of the plantation. Historians think that it may have been placed there by slaves as a secret religious act to either cast a spell or offer a blessing for the house's occupants.

Following the Civil War, many of the freed slaves chose to remain and continue to work on the plantation land. Today, Stagville is an historic 70-acre site owned by the State of North Carolina with a few of the nineteenth-century buildings still standing. It hosts a series of seminars, workshops and conferences on historic preservation and African-American studies.

FAYETTEVILLE

Evans Metropolitan Methodist Church—301 Cool Spring St. (919) 483-2862. This was the first Methodist church in Fayetteville, built in 1803 by black minister Rev. Henry Evans.

Fayetteville State University—1200 Murchison Rd. (919) 486-1111. This school was originally called Fayetteville Teacher's College and was founded by seven local blacks determined to have their children well educated. It is considered the oldest normal school for both blacks and whites in the South.

GREENSBORO

Greensboro—The town of Greensboro was the site of several civil rights protest sit-ins during the early 1960s which began when four black college students refused to move from a Greensboro Woolworth's lunch counter after they were denied service.

Mattye Reed African Heritage Center—1601 E. Market St. on the main campus of the North Carolina A&T State University. (919) 334-7874. Hours: Mon.-Fri. 9-12, 2:30-3:30, or by appointment. The Reed Center has a significant collection of more than 6,000 items from 35 African countries, New Guinea and Haiti. Most of the artifacts are functional—baskets, bowls, dishes, weapons and fabrics—and represent the traditional and contemporary lifestyles of African cultures. The center's permanent collection also includes African masks, icons, bronze, ivory and wood sculptures. It regularly offers tours, lectures, seminars, music workshops, and slide shows.

North Carolina Agricultural & Technological State University—East Market St. (919) 334-7500. Then known as the Agricultural and Mechanical College for the Colored Race, this school began in 1890 as an extension of Shaw University. Its African Heritage Museum has a substantial collection of sculptures and basket works from West and Central Africa.

RALEIGH

John Chavis Memorial Park—East Lenoir and Worth Sts. A park dedicated to John Chavis, a free black teacher and Presbyterian minister who was educated at Princeton University. During the early 1800s, Chavis taught and preached to both blacks and whites in the Raleigh area. Following the Nat Turner Rebellion, Chavis was forced to give up his ministry and stop teaching black students. A plaque in the park honors his work.

North Carolina Museum of Art—2110 Blue Ridge Blvd. off I-40, Wade Avenue exit. (919) 833-1935. Hours: Tues.-Sat. 9-5, Fri. 9-9, Sun. noon-5. A museum dedicated to the historic stages of art throughout the world, its collection includes African art and sculptures, along with pieces from ancient Egypt.

North Carolina Museum of History—109 E. Jones St. (919) 733-3894. Hours: Tues.-Sat. 9-5, Sun. 1-6. Dedicated to the history of North Carolina, this museum includes a collection of hand-crafted furniture produced by black cabinet maker Thomas Day. A free black, Day owned his own factory in Milton, North Carolina, where he employed both black and white carpenters. His furniture was so highly regarded that when he chose to move out of Milton because black laws did not allow him to bring his wife (a free black woman) into the state, the people of Milton were granted a special exemption for Mrs. Day from the legislature.

St. Augustine's College—1315 Oakwood Ave. (919) 828-4451. Founded by the Protestant Episcopal Church in 1867 for blacks. This Southern-style, tree-shaded 110-acre campus includes several buildings that are listed on the National Register of Historic Places including Taylor Hall and the college chapel.

Shaw University—118 East South St. (919) 755-4800. Established in 1865 by a frugal Civil War veteran who saved his army pay, a woolen goods manufacturer, and the Freedmen's Bureau, Shaw University was one of the first schools in the U.S. dedicated to training black lawyers and doctors. Campus buildings are an eclectic collection of historic and modern.

ROANOKE ISLAND

North Carolina Aquarium for Roanoke Island—Airport Rd. at Mateo. (919) 473-3493. Mon.-Sat., 9-5, Sun. 1-5. In addition to the natural history displays of North Carolina fish, turtles and other sea animals, this aquarium features a small display in honor of Captain Richard Etheridge. Born on Roanoke Island, Etheridge was a former slave who went on to become the first black commander of the Pea Island Lifesaving Station. The exhibit depicts the story of Etheridge's life and the history of the Pea Island station until its closing in 1952. The exhibit occasionally travels to other sites, so phone ahead before visiting.

ROCKY MOUNT

Dred Wimberly Memorial—816 North Raleigh St. In the town often called the "Capital of Gospel Singers," this memorial honors Dred Wimberly, a former slave who served as a state representative in 1879 and as a state senator in 1889.

SALISBURY

Livingstone College—West Monroe St. (704) 638-5500. Hours: daily 9-4:30. Founded in 1879 by the eloquent black orator and leader Dr. Joseph Charles Price. Livingstone hosted the first black inter-collegiate football game on the campus lawn in 1892. The W.J. Walls Heritage Hall has an African culture room, a black history room, and paintings and documents relating to the A.M.E. Zion Church. Some of the African artifacts in the museum were collected by Bishop W.J. Walls while on his travels through Africa.

SEDALIA

Charlotte Hawkins Brown Memorial State Historic Site—In the Palmer Institute, 6135 Burlington Rd., east of Greensboro via I-85, take exit 135 north or US 70 east from Greensboro. (919) 449-4846. Hours: Tues.-Sat. 10-4, Sun. 1-4 p.m. North Carolina's first state historic site honoring an African-American, it is dedicated to Charlotte "Lottie" Hawkins, the granddaughter of slaves who established a day and boarding school for black students in 1902. Hawkins also ran the Palmer Institute in Sedalia for 50 years and brought national acclaim to it for its vocational training, cultural education, and emphasis on the individual worth of each student. The Palmer Institute stopped functioning as a vocational school in 1961, but today offers educational exhibits, presentations and tours.

WINSTON SALEM

Delta Art Center - 1511 East Third St. (919) 722-2625. Hours: Mon.-Fri. 10-5:30. Rotating exhibits, lectures, and workshops created with the black perspective in mind. Sponsored by Winston-Salem Delta Fine Arts, Inc., the organization which sponsored the purchase of the Thomas Day Collection at the North Carolina Museum of History, established a permanent collection of black art at the Winston-Salem State University, and is dedicated to the preservation of North Carolina black culture.

Museum of Early Southern Decorative Arts—924 South Main St. within the Old Salem Restoration. (919) 721-7360. Hours: 10:30-4:30, Sun. 1:30-4:30. A museum devoted to the collection and study of Southern decorative art created before 1821. The museum includes the works of many black artisans—historians say that there were almost 3,000 black artisans in the state during the early 1800s—who worked as silversmiths, potters, weavers, and woodcarvers, but for the most part their names are unknown.

WASHINGTON, D.C.

Along with being one of the most beautiful and cosmopolitan cities in the world, full of marble monuments and historic tree-lined neighborhoods, Washington, D.C., has one of the most vibrant and influential black communities in the United States. For over 200 years, prominent African-American men and women have been leaving their mark on the nation's capital.

Although most of the earliest blacks in the area were brought there as slaves to pave the streets and construct government buildings, one outstanding black figure in the 1700s rose well above most in terms of public achievement. Benjamin Banneker, a noted mathematician and astronomer whose father was a former slave, was called upon to assist Pierre L'Enfant with the city's original design. When L'Enfant was relieved of his architectural duties and took all the copies of the plans back to Paris, Secretary of State Thomas Jefferson called on Banneker, who memorized the plans, to reconstruct them.

In 1800, the 3,200 black slaves in Washington represented 80 percent of the black population. By 1830, 6,000 black slaves were matched by 6,000 free blacks. During the War of 1812, blacks went to battle for their city along with whites. In 1815, after the city was severely damaged by the British, slaves helped rebuild the ruins. In the years that followed, the small community of free blacks started to develop their own network of churches, schools, and businesses.

During the 1830s slavery was still the norm and white animosity was a constant. In 1835, the Snow Riots erupted when gangs of whites destroyed many homes, schools and churches in the black community in an attempt to stifle the abolitionist cause. But blacks continued to stream into the city seeking the freedom and opportunities they were denied in the Deep South.

At the start of the Civil War, 80 percent of the city's blacks were free. Following the war, Washington's black population grew rapidly as thousands of freed slaves fled the Southern states. Many whites in the South were outraged by what they considered to be Washington's solicitous treatment of its black community.

In 1862 emancipation was granted by Congress and soon after public schools for blacks began to be established. Black citizens were appointed to public office and the segregation of public accommodations became prohibited. By 1870, the black population represented one-third of the city's population and urban ghettos swelled with the new arrivals.

During Reconstruction a certain amount of progress was made—black newspapers were founded, and blacks were appointed to federal offices—but soon after Congress started pulling in the reins and took back the control black Washingtonians had gained. By 1900 the city was again segregated.

In 1919 angry white gangs terrorized the city's black neighborhoods in an attack on what they called rampant "black criminality." The violence aggravated race relations and led to the 1925 Ku Klux Klan parade at the Washington Monument.

But the 1920s also brought a small amount of progress to Washington's black community. In the Shaw neighborhood of the city, on what was then called the "Black Broadway," the Howard and Lincoln Theaters brought some of the country's finest entertainers to Washington's black society. Both were grand showplaces that hosted jazz greats including Duke Ellington, who was born in Washington as the son of a White House butler. Also at this time there developed in Washington a small segment of the black population who managed to overcome the obstacles and grow in economic and professional status; a community of lawyers, doctors, and educators prospered.

The Great Depression that brought gloom to the rest of the country actually brought slight improvement for Washington's blacks. Federal agencies eased their hiring policies in favor of blacks, and Franklin D. Roosevelt formed his so-called "Black Cabinet."

The 1930s brought a modicum of educational achievement; blacks were admitted to the graduate programs of American and Catholic Universities. In 1939, contralto Marian Anderson, after being denied permission to perform at Constitution Hall because she was black, attracted national civil rights attention when she gave a much-heralded public performance at the Lincoln Memorial.

Following World War II, Washington's black community joined forces in a series of demonstrations and boycotts that brought the removal of many of the city's racial restrictions. Although still economically deprived, the community was now demanding equal opportunities in housing, education and access to public places.

In 1954 desegregation of the city's public schools began and much of the inner city white population dwindled in response. As elsewhere in the country, the 1960s brought a great deal of strife with the pursuit of civil rights. The assassination of Martin Luther King, Jr., in Memphis in 1968, touched off six days of rioting in the capital. Large areas of the city's black sections were looted and burned before calm was restored.

Although Washington today, with a population that is about three-fourths black, is one of the most advanced cities in the country in regard to racial equality, many of its neighborhoods remain racially exclusive. The middle-class sections are the most racially mixed; the poorest ones are almost all black, and the most affluent ones are still predominantly white. But Washington does boast of having the highest percentage of black college graduates of any major city in the United States, and it is home to the largest and one of the most prestigious black schools in the country, Howard University. It has also had two black mayors overseeing its community's politics.

WASHINGTON, D.C. SITES

For general travel information contact the Washington, D.C., Convention & Visitors Association: 1212 New York Ave. N.W., Washington, D.C. 20005. (202) 789-7000.

For a free brochure on the Washington, D.C., Black History National Recreational Trail, a series of sites that illustrate many aspects of black history in the area, contact: National Parks Service, National Capital Region, Office of Public Affairs, 1100 Ohio Dr., S.W., Washington, D.C. 20242, (202) 485-9666.

Anacostia Museum—(Smithsonian Institute) 1901 Fort Place, S.E. in Fort Stanton Park. (202) 287-3369. Hours:

daily 10-5. An impressive museum that also serves as a national research center devoted to African-American history and culture. Exhibits change regularly and include themes such as music, art, literature, people and the African continent. Guided tours offered on weekdays.

Anthony Bowen YMCA—1325 W St. N.W. (202) 462-1054. Hours: Mon.-Fri. 7a.m.-8p.m., Sat.-Sun. 9a.m.-4p.m. Two years after the first YMCA was established in Boston, a former slave turned prominent educator, Anthony Bowen, founded the first YMCA for blacks in the world here in Washington. After being moved to several locations and then being closed by city officials in 1982, it was transferred to this site in 1987 and currently offers programs for Shaw neighborhood youths.

Association for the Study of Afro-American Life and History—1407 14th St. N.W. (202) 667-2822. Hours: Mon.-Fri. 9-5. Founded by historian Dr. Carter G. Woodson in 1915, who was one of the first black historians to devote his life to the documentation of black history in America, the association serves as a library, archive repository and research center for information on black history. The association also publishes periodicals on black history including the *Journal of Negro History*.

Banneker Circle & Fountain—L'Enfant Plaza near Main Ave. and Water St. in southwest Washington. A memorial park dedicated to black mathematician and astronomer Benjamin Banneker. The self-taught son of a former slave, Banneker constructed the first wooden clock and was co-designer of the city of Washington in 1791.

Bethune Museum & Archives—1318 Vermont Ave. N.W. (202) 322-1233. Hours: Mon.-Fri. 8-5. A center for black women's history housed in the fully restored nineteenth-century home of noted black educator and civil rights activist Mary McLeod Bethune. Formerly the headquarters of the National Council of Negro Women which was founded by Bethune, the museum consists of five galleries that house archives, photographs, paintings, and documents relating to the history of black women in America.

Blues Alley—1073 Rear Wisconsin Ave. N.W. in Georgetown. (202) 337-4141. Hours: Sun.-Thurs. 6p.m.-midnight, Fri.-Sat 6p.m.-2a.m. One of the best-known clubs in D.C., Blues Alley has been dazzling audiences with national Dixieland, blues and jazz acts for over 25 years. At least two shows are offered each night.

Capitol Entertainment Services—3629 18th St. N.E. (202) 636-9203. Offers a regularly scheduled "Black History Tour" that includes the Frederick Douglass National Historic Home, National Museum of African Art, Mary McLeod Bethune Memorial, and the National Portrait Gallery.

Decatur House—748 Jackson Pl., N.W. (202) 842-0920. Hours: Tues.-Fri. 10-2, Sat.-Sun. noon-4. One of Washington's oldest and most elegant Victorian-style homes, built in 1819, the Decatur House was sold to infamous slave trader John Gadsby in the 1830s. Gadsby kept his slaves, who later were sent to Georgia, in the house attic. Historians have written that their cries of anguish could be heard from the street outside all night long. Tours are offered on the half-hour.

Duke Ellington Birthplace—2129 Ward Pl. N.W. A modern office building now stands on this site where the great jazz musician was born. A simple plaque that reads "DUKE ELLINGTON BUILDING" marks the spot.

Duke Ellington Childhood Home—1212 T St. N.W. Not

open to the public. This Shaw neighborhood row house, where Ellington grew up, was one of the many stately T Street homes owned by middle class blacks in the early 1900s. It was here that Ellington took his earliest piano lessons, played baseball, and worked as a soda jerk after school in a nearby shop.

Duke Ellington School of the Arts—35th and R Sts. N.W., in Georgetown. (202) 282-0123. A D.C. public high school named for the noted Washington native, this four-year pre-professional school specializes in training in drama, dance, vocals and instrumental music. Entrance standards are high and most students continue on to other fine schools and pursue careers in the arts.

Emancipation Proclamation—Library of Congress, 1st and Capitol Streets, S.E. (202) 287-5000. Hours: Mon- Fri. 8:30 a.m.-5 p.m., Sat.-Sun. 8:30-6. A permanent exhibit that houses the first draft of the historic proclamation that led to the abolition of slavery.

Emancipation Memorial—E. Capitol Street between 11th and 13th Sts. N.E. in Lincoln Park. A bronze statue that depicts Archer Alexander, the last man captured under the Fugitive Slave Law, as he breaks free from his shackles, and President Lincoln holding the Emancipation Proclamation.

Ebenezer Methodist Church—4th and D Sts., S.E., (202) 554-1415. Founded in 1805, this church was the former site of the first public school for blacks in Washington.

Evans-Tibbs Collection—1910 Vermont Ave., N.W. (202) 234-8164. Hours: Wed.-Thurs. 6-8 p.m., Sat. 2-5 p.m. Housed in the former home of the first black professional opera singer Lillian Evans-Tibbs, this museum collection includes paintings and sculptures by eighteenth, nineteenth and twentieth century African-American artists.

Frederick Douglass Memorial Home—1411 W St., S.E. (202) 426-5960. Hours: Daily 9-4. Former home of the noted black abolitionist, orator, diplomat, writer, and auditor of the Treasury. The home is decorated with period antiques and appears as it did when Douglass lived there.

Howard Theater—624 T St. N.W. in the Shaw neighborhood. This Italian Renaissance theater built in 1920 was the first legitimate theater for blacks in Washington. Second in status to Harlem's Apollo Theater, the Howard was once a grand arena where Washington's black society turned out for national musical acts. In its early days performers included Ethel Waters, Duke Ellington, Ella Fitzgerald, Dinah Washington, Lionel Hampton, and Washington native Pearl Bailey. In later years it hosted Diana Ross and the Supremes, Smokey Robinson, and Marvin Gaye. Closed in 1970, the Howard currently stands in deteriorated condition.

Howard University—2400 6th St., N.W. (202) 686-5400. Founded in 1867 and named for General Oliver Otis Howard, Howard University is one of the most prestigious, historically black universities in the country. Its alumni have included Supreme Court Justice Thurgood Marshall and Atlanta Mayor Andrew Young. The university's Moorland-Spingarn Research Center houses the largest collection of literature on African-American topics in the country. And its Gallery of Fine Arts houses the permanent Alain Locke African collection.

James Reese Europe Birthplace—1008 S St. N.W. Not open to the public. Childhood home of James Reese Europe, the nation's first African-American bandleader who entertained World War I troops with ragtime, blues, jazz, and spirituals. Reese is buried in Arlington National Cemetery.

Lincoln Memorial—On the Mall in Potomac Park. Site of the 1939 Easter Sunday recital by black contralto Marian Anderson who sang operatic arias and spirituals at the memorial after being denied permission to perform at Constitution Hall because of her race. Also the site of the historic August 28, 1963, "I Have a Dream" speech by Dr. Martin Luther King, Jr.

Lincoln Park—Along East Capitol St. between 11th and 13th Sts. N.E. This park celebrates the abolition of slavery in the nation's capital. The park's Abraham Lincoln statue, dedicated in 1876, was paid for solely with funds donated by freed slaves. In 1974, a statue of Mary McLeod Bethune was erected by the National Council of Negro Women.

Lincoln Theater—1215 U St., N.W. (202) 462-4591 (Lincoln Theater Foundation). Currently under renovation. U Street between 1920 and the 1950s was known as Washington's "black Broadway" and the Lincoln Theater, a Georgian Revival structure built in 1921, was its focal point. It was here that Duke Ellington, Billie Holiday, Count Bassie, and Cab Calloway performed.

Malcom X Park—16th St. between Florida Ave. and Euclid St., N.W (Officially called Meridian Hill Park.) A 12-acre park that during the 1960s served as a meeting place and forum for civil rights groups, the park was unofficially dedicated to the slain black nationalist leader after his death.

Martin Luther King, Jr., Memorial Library—901 G St., N.W. (202) 727-1221. Hours: Mon.-Sat. 9-5:30, Sun. 1-5 (Closed Sundays in summer). The main branch of the city's public library, facilities include an archive collection of the city's history, a black studies division, and a lobby mural depicting the life and legacy of Dr. Martin Luther King, Jr.

Mayfair Mansions—West of Kenilworth Ave., between Jay and Hayes Sts., N.E. Built in 1942, the Mayfair Gardens, as it was originally called consisted of 17 three-story luxury buildings constructed for black families who were uprooted due to nearby federal construction. Designed by black architect Albert I. Cassell, the project was the first federally subsidized black housing complex in the country. Currently, Mayfair Mansions is one of the largest apartment complexes for low- to moderate income families in Washington.

Metropolitan A.M.E. Church—1518 M St. N.W. (202) 331-1246. Hours: Mon.-Fri. 10-4, services on Sunday at 8 and 11. A downtown architectural landmark that was built by slaves and former slaves, this church, whose roots date back to 1822, was the first A.M.E church established in D.C. With a seating capacity of 2,500, it is considered the national cathedral of the A.M.E. Church in America. Parishioners have included Frederick Douglass and educator Francis Cardozo. Presidents McKinley, Theodore Roosevelt, and Taft addressed meetings here, and in 1942 Eleanor Roosevelt delivered a moving address on the importance of ending racism in America.

Mt. Zion Cemetery/Female Union Band Cemetery—Behind 2515-2531 Q St. N.W., near the Mt. Zion United Methodist Church. These two cemeteries form the oldest, predominantly black burial grounds in D.C. Historians say that the grounds once served as a hiding place for slaves utilizing the Underground Railroad. Although in neglected condition, many of the historic markers are under restoration.

National Museum of African Art—(Smithsonian Institute) 950 Independence Ave., S.W. (202) 375-2700. Hours: daily 10-5:30. The only museum in America devoted solely to the art and culture of Africa. Permanent exhibits include the role of art in African society, ceremonial religious masks, and the traditional arts of sub-Saharan Africa.

National Museum of American History—(Smithsonian Institute) 14th St. and Constitution Ave. N.W. (202) 357-2700. Hours: daily 10-5:30. In addition to a general exhibit on American history, the museum houses a second floor exhibit on African-American migration, and several other exhibits that relate to black history and culture.

National Museum of American Art—8th and G Sts. N.W., in the Old Patent Office Building. (202) 357-1300. Hours: daily 10-5:30. Over 1,400 works by African-American artists, including a special gallery of works by nineteenth-century African-American artists.

National Museum of Natural History—Constitution Ave. at 10th St., N.W., (202) 357-2700. Hours: daily 10-5:30. An array of exhibits that focus on the natural surroundings of vast cultures, with one of the most colorful being African Hall, a display of traditional life in rural Africa.

National Portrait Gallery—8th and F Sts N.W. in the Old Patent Office Building. (202) 357-1300. Hours: daily 10-5:30. The museum holds a special collection of portraits of members of the Harlem Renaissance period in addition to a collection of works by black artists.

National Theater—1321 Pennsylvania Ave. N.W. (202) 628-3393. Washington's oldest continuously operating theater, the National Theater, founded in 1835, has historic significance to American blacks. During its early history, the theater refused entry to blacks, and by the 1920s and 1930s it was a focal point of anti-segregation protests in the city. For a while it hosted so-called "Black Days," permitting blacks to attend performances by black entertainers on specific days only. In 1952, pressured by civil rights policies, the theater opened its doors to all races.

Phillips Collection—1600-1612 21st St. N.W. (202) 387-0961. Hours: Tues.-Sat 10-5, Sun. 2-7. A vast collection housed in the Victorian brownstone home of the late Duncan Phillips that includes "Migration of the Negro," a 30-panel display done by Harlem Renaissance artist Jacob Lawrence

Ralph Bunche Home—1510 Jackson St. N.E. in Brookland. Not open to the public. Built in 1941, this was the home of noted black scholar and diplomat Ralph Bunche and his family while he taught at Howard University. Bunche conducted research with Swedish sociologist Gunnar Myrdal on race relations in America, served as the U.N. Secretary General's representative, and in 1950 was the first black awarded the Nobel Prize for Peace.

Shaw Neighborhood—In the northwest quadrant of the city. A predominantly black residential neighborhood today, Shaw from the 1920s to the 1940s was a bustling business and social district for Washington's black commuity. It also was a childhood home for many of Washington's famous blacks. Like Harlem, it had several influential churches, along with many businesses, pool halls, bars and nightclubs, including the grand Howard and Lincoln theaters. During the 1968 riots, several parts of the neighborhood were destroyed.

St. Luke's Episcopal Church—1514 15th St. N.W. (202) 667-4394. Founded in 1879 by noted orator and champion of black solidarity Rev. Alexander Crummell, St. Luke's was the first independent black Episcopal church in Washington. Crummell, who was a descendant of African royalty, founded the American Negro Academy. The church, constructed out of local bluestone in country-Gothic style, was designed by Washington's first black architect, Calvin T.S. Brent. Services are still held.

Tidal Basin Bridge—Near the Thomas Jefferson Memorial in West Potomac Park, this bridge was designed by the prominent black engineer and architect Archie A. Alexander.

Whitelaw Hotel—1839 13th St. N.W. in the Shaw neighborhood. Built in 1910 and named for its builder, black entrepreneur John Whitelaw Lewis, this gray brick hotel was once the only large hotel in Washington that accepted black guests. Patrons included George Washington Carver, Joe Lewis and Cab Calloway. Once the scene of elegant parties and balls, the Whitelaw fell into decline by the 1960s and was closed by the city in 1977. A Georgia businessman recently purchased the property with plans of restoring the hotel to its original condition.

WPFW-FM 'Bama Hour—Considered a local Washington legend, WPFW radio station's *'Bama Hour* is a favorite of both the black and white communities. Hosted by Jerry Washington, a flamboyant character with a soulful drawl, the *'Bama* Hour is a three-hour show full of soul, blues and jazz, along with plenty obscure small talk. Along with call-ins from listeners, it occasionally invites city and national figures as guests. It airs from 11a.m. to 2p.m. on Saturday.

VIRGINIA

*A*s the northernmost of the Southern states, Virginia has a relatively small amount of the traditional, Deep South character that permeates its southern neighbors, but its early history is one steeped in the story of slavery.

In 1612, Virginia began cultivating its first commercial tobacco farms, just four years after the English colonists settled at Jamestown. Blacks first arrived as indentured servants in Virginia in 1619. By the 1640s, as the lucrative tobacco farms began to develop on both sides of the James River, the importation of much-needed West African slaves had become established in the colony.

The 1700s are what historians call Virginia's golden age. An aristocratic planter society, made up of about 350 families, held a monopoly on the political and economic control of the region. In English country-gentry tradition, they lived in comfortable splendor and multiplied their wealth by speculating in land and slave-trading.

In 1700, Virginia was the largest of the English colonies with a population of about 75,000. Blacks, mostly slaves, constituted 50 percent of the total population of Williamsburg. When the tidewater and lower Piedmont tobacco plantations began to represent greater and greater economic prosperity for the area, the demand for slaves continued to grow. As the slave population increased, blacks lived together in larger numbers on plantations and in towns, forming a distinct network of African-American culture and traditions.

During the early 1800s, many of the vast tobacco fields were exhausted, and the planters tried to use them for cotton in order to rejuvenate the land. In an effort to improve their economic condition which was on a slight decline, the planters turned to the slave trade to supplement their income. By the mid-1800s Virginia was known throughout the country as the "breeder of slaves." A former slave auction block in Fredericksburg is now an historic site and tourist attraction.

Following the War of 1812, the western counties of the state spoke out in favor of freeing slaves, but the eastern counties were opposed. All hope for the freeing of slaves ended in 1831 when Nat Turner and about 60 of his fellow slaves tried to instigate a slave revolt in Southampton County. The insurrection resulted in 57 whites being killed. When it was over, Nat Turner was hung. After the Turner massacre, opposition to slavery in the state faded away and stricter slave codes were enforced. For the most part, Virginia maintained a pro-slavery position that was hostile to Northern abolitionists.

In 1856, Booker T. Washington, noted author, educator and presidential adviser, was born in Hardy. Washington lived and worked as a slave for the first nine years of his life at Burroughs Plantation. Washington's Burroughs Plantation homesite is now a national monument.

The North/South clash intensified in 1859 with John Brown's raid on Harper's Ferry. Brown and several followers, including five blacks, seized the U.S. arsenal at Harper's Ferry (now in West Virginia) in an attempt to persuade slaves to rise up against their owners.

Brown was taken prisoner and hanged. The raid, and Brown's execution, drove pro-slavery and anti-slavery groups farther apart.

In 1861, the first black men were enlisted in the Union navy at Fort Monroe. Also in 1861 Virginia seceded from the Union, and went on to become the center of military and political operations during the Civil War. Over half of all Civil War battles were fought on Virginia land. Following the war Virginia's economy was in shambles and its much needed black work force had uncertain status. Over 350,000 Virginia slaves were freed, and much of the plantation aristocracy longed for the good old days of guaranteed slave labor.

Recently freed slaves voted in large numbers in 1867 state elections. In 1868 Hampton University was established for the education of freed slaves. But in 1902 conservative white politicians imposed a new constitution that enacted poll taxes and literacy tests in order to disenfranchise black voters.

The U.S. Supreme Court desegregation decision of 1954 dominated state politics for a decade. Senator Byrd pushed through the General Assembly a policy of "massive resistance" in an effort to maintain segregation. In the years that followed few schools were desegregated and many of those that had been were forced to close.

The 1965 Civil Rights Voting Act permitted federal examiners to register blacks under certain circumstances, and in 1966 the U.S. Supreme Court struck down Virginia's poll tax in state elections. At the end of the 1960s all school districts were at least partially integrated.

By the 1970s most of the Old South solidarity had dissipated, and many blacks were elected to local government. In 1977, a black majority was elected to the Richmond city council, and a black mayor was elected.

In 1989, L. Douglas Wilder, born the grandson of freed slaves in Richmond, was elected governor, the first black man in United States history to hold such a distinction.

VIRGINIA SITES

For general travel information contact the Virginia Division of Tourism: 1021 East Carey St., Richmond, VA, 23219. (804) 786-4484

ALEXANDRIA

The Alexandria Black History Resource Center—638 North Alfred St. (703) 838-4356. Hours: Tues.-Sat. 10-4. A black history museum that portrays the contributions of African-Americans to Alexandria's history and culture. Included are photographs, paintings, memorabilia, lectures, events, and walking tours of nearby black historic sites.

Alfred Street Baptist Church—301 S. Alfred St. (703) 683-2222. An historic black church that still holds Sunday services.

APPOMATTOX

Appomattox Courthouse National Historical Park— Three miles northeast of Appomattox on VA 24. (703) 352-8987. Hours: daily 9-5. A reconstructed building that now serves as a museum and visitor center, the Appomattox Courthouse is the site where in 1865 General Robert E. Lee surrendered to General Ulysses S. Grant, bringing an end to the Civil War. During the summer, the museum and village stage a dramatic reenactment that highlights the roles of free blacks in the area during the Civil War.

ARLINGTON

Arlington National Cemetery—Eisenhower Dr. (703) 692-0931. Hours: daily 8-5. Narrated bus tours leave from the cemetery's visitor center and points of interest include the gravesite of Medgar Evers, the civil rights leader from Mississippi whose murder prompted President John F. Kennedy to forward the congressional bill that guaranteed equal rights in public accommodations.

Dr. Charles Richard Drew's Home—2505 First St. South. A National Historic Landmark that is not open to the public, this was the home of Charles R. Drew, the black physician noted for discovering a method to preserve blood plasma.

CHARLOTTESVILLE

Ash Lawn-Highland—On CR 795 about two miles past Monticello. (804) 293-9539. Hours: daily 9-5. Home of President James Monroe who played a key role in the 1821 founding of the African nation of Liberia, where the capital city, Monrovia, bares his name. The creation of Liberia began as an experiment that was to repatriate former slaves to their ancestral home. Today, Ash Lawn-Highland is a museum estate with a slave cabin still intact.

Monticello—Off I-64, 1/2 mile south on VA 20 and 1 1/2 miles east on VA 53. (804) 295-8181. Hours: daily 9-4:30. The historic home of President Thomas Jefferson who was publicly opposed to slavery but utilized slave labor to build this magnificent estate. Tours of the property include slave quarters and an account of the important role black servants played in the running of the plantation.

Thomas Jefferson Visitors Center—Off I-64 on VA 20.

(804) 293-6789. Hours: daily 9-5. Included in this information center on President Thomas Jefferson is an exhibit that portrays the lives of black servants who lived on his estate.

CLARKSVILLE

Prestwood Plantation—Hwy. 15 North. (804) 374-8672. Hours: daily 9-5 April-October. An eighteenth-century plantation that features the oldest standing slave house in the country, along with a slave cemetery, loom house and plantation store.

FREDERICKSBURG

Fredericksburg Tourist Bureau—706 Caroline St. (703) 373-1776. Hours: daily 9-5. The bureau offers free pamphlets on the black history of Fredericksburg with a listing of black heritage walking tours.

Shiloh Old Site Baptist Church—801 Sophia St. (703) 373-8701. Currently called the African Baptist Church, during the 1800s the Shiloh Church had a white, free black, and slave congregation. The church's minister Lawrence A. Davies was elected the first black mayor of Fredericksburg in 1976.

Slave Auction Block—At the corner of Charles and William Sts. Site of pre-Civil War Fredericksburg slave auctions.

HAMPTON

Fort Monroe Casemate Museum—Casemate 20 on Bernard Rd. (804) 727-3391. Hours: daily 9-5. A permanent exhibit on the slaves who escaped to Fort Monroe during the Civil War, one year before the Emancipation Proclamation, and were declared contraband of war by Union

General Benjamin Butler. The former slaves worked at building roads and fortifications in the Hampton area.

Hampton University—Marshall Dr. (804) 727-5000. Founded in 1868 for the education of freed slaves, Hampton University graduated Booker T. Washington. Guided tours of the campus are available, and the Hampton University Museum (Hours: Mon.-Fri. 8-5, Sat.-Sun. 12-4) showcases a collection of art and artifacts from African and African-American artists. The Collis P. Huntington Memorial Library on campus houses one of the oldest collections of black history artifacts in the country including original slave handbills and personal papers of Booker T. Washington, Mary McLeod Bethune, and George Washington Carver.

HARDY

Booker T. Washington National Monument—17 miles southeast of Roanoke on Rt. 3. (703) 721-2094. Hours: daily 8:30-5. Birthplace of Booker T. Washington, where he lived on the Burroughs Plantation as a slave. The memorial and visitors center include reconstructed slave cabins, a blacksmith shed, and barns for tobacco and horses. Tours are available, and in summer months costumed dramas are performed.

JAMESTOWN

Jamestown Settlement Museum—Rt. 31 and Colonial Pkwy. next to Jamestown Island. (804) 229-1607. Hours: daily 9-5. An exhibit that tells the story of the Virginia colony from its founding in 1607 to 1699 that includes the role of blacks in seventeenth-century Virginia. It was in Jamestown, in August of 1619, that blacks first arrived in America as indentured servants on a Dutch ship. Many of these black servants bought their freedom and owned land of their own before they were forced into slavery in 1669. The museum features replicas of the ships that brought the settlers and blacks to Jamestown, artifacts, art, life-size statues, and a live history performance of colonial life by costumed interpreters.

MOUNT VERNON

Mount Vernon Estate—At the southern end of George Washington Memorial Pkwy., 16 miles south of Alexandria. (703) 780-2000. Hours: daily 9-5. The home and burial site of President George Washington, Mount Vernon Estate once employed over 300 slaves who worked as blacksmiths, gardeners, brickmakers, herdsmen, shoemakers, spinners, weavers, distillers, and boatmen. President Washington, unlike many other plantation owners, supplied medical care for his slaves, recognized marriages between them, and in his will provided freedom for them upon his death. Today, the estate offers tours of the home, working areas, slave quarters, and nearby slave burial grounds.

NEWPORT NEWS

War Memorial Museum of Virginia—9285 Warwick Blvd. in Huntington Park. (804) 247-8523. Hours: Mon.-Sat. 9-5, Sun 1-5. A museum dedicated to U.S. military history since 1775 with the largest collection of military memorabilia in the country. A special exhibit focuses on the role of blacks in U.S. military history including a tribute to the all-black 10th Cavalry which fought in the Spanish-American War.

NORFOLK

Elmwood Cemetery—On Princess Anne Rd. (804) 441-2653. Hours: daily 9-5. The cemetery includes gravestones of black soldiers and sailors who died in the Civil War and the Spanish-American War, and a granite memorial to black veterans of the Civil War.

PETERSBURG

First Baptist Church—228-242 Harrison St. (804) 732-2841. The earliest African-American church established in the U.S. Services still held.

Joseph Jenkins Roberts Monument—Halifax and South Sycamore Sts. A monument in honor of Joseph Jenkins Roberts, a prominent black merchant who left Petersburg to become the first president of the new west African nation of Liberia which was founded by free blacks and the American Colonization Society in 1817.

Petersburg National Battlefield Park—On Rt. 36, two miles east of Petersburg. Hours:8 a.m.-dusk. A 1,500-acre park with historic exhibits that preserve the site where in 1864 General Grant encircled Petersburg forcing the surrender of the Confederate soldiers. The 10-month siege involved 32 black infantry regiments and two black cavalry units among the troops. The 48th Pennsylvania Infantry, consisting mainly of black coal miners, dug a tunnel beneath the Confederate lines and filled it with explosives. The detonation created a huge crater, part of which is still visible in the park, and killed or injured 3,798 men.

PORTSMOUTH

Virginia Sports Hall of Fame—420 High St. (804) 393-8031. Hours: Tues.-Sat. 10-5, Sun. 1-5. Sports memorabilia and exhibits on American athletes, including black athletes Arthur Ashe, Jr., Roosevelt Brown, and Leroy Keyes.

RICHMOND

Bill "Bojangles" Robinson Statue—At the corner of Adams and Leigh Sts. In honor of the acclaimed star who lived in Richmond.

Black History Museum and Cultural Center of Virginia—00 Clay St. (804) 780-9093. Hours: Tues., Thurs., Fri., Sat. 11-4. A museum dedicated to the documentation of black history, business, education and politics in Virginia from 1607 to the present.

Jackson Ward District—The northside of Broad St. west of the capitol building. This 22-block area, often called the "Wall Street of Black America," is a designated National Historic Landmark. One of the oldest black neighborhoods in the U.S., it includes over 100 pre-Civil War buildings, and the country's first black-owned bank and insurance companies.

Maggie L. Walker National Historic Site—110 1/2 East Leigh St. (804) 780-1380. Hours: Wed.-Sun. 9-5. Home of Maggie L. Walker, civic leader, newspaper editor, and the first black woman in the U.S. to establish and preside over her own bank. The restored 22-room home is furnished with many original antiques.

Richmond National Battlefield Park—3215 E. Broad St. (809) 226-1981. An outdoor exhibit at the park depicts the contributions of thousands of black soldiers. Park grounds are the site of many Civil War battles between 1864 and 1865 including one in which a brigade of black troops helped Union forces take control of Confederate Fort Harrison.

Task Force For Historic Preservation and The Minority Community—500 N. 3 St. (804) 788-1709. Hours: daily 9-5. A cultural center and historical society that houses documents and artifacts that relate to black history of Virginia and the U.S.

Valentine Museum—1015 E. Clay St. (804) 649-0711. Hours: Mon.-Sat. 10-5, Sun. 12-5. The life and history of Richmond is the focus of this museum, which dedicates several exhibits throughout the year to African-American history of the area.

Virginia Museum of Fine Arts—2800 Grove Ave. (804) 367-0844. Hours: Tues.-Sat. 11-5, Thurs. 11-10, Sun. 1-5. One of the South's finest museums with a permanent collection of African art.

ROANOKE

Harrison Museum of African-American Culture—523 Harrison Ave. N.W. (703) 345-4818. Hours: Mon.-Fri. 10-5. A museum dedicated to the preservation and interpretation of black heritage in southwestern Virginia.

WASHINGTON'S BIRTHPLACE

George Washington's Birthplace Pope's Creek Plantation—Washington's Birthplace in eastern Virginia. (804) 224-1732. Hours: daily 9-5. Pope's Creek Plantation was where George Washington was born in 1732 and lived until he was three years old. The stately brick home burned to the ground in 1779, and on its site the National Parks Service has recreated the living quarters of a relatively privileged female house servant as part of an exhibit on slave life at Pope's Creek. The female slave's personal possessions included a mattress and bolster, two blankets and an extra set of clothing, all considered a privilege at the time. Her high position in the plantation hierarchy is exhibited by a tin cup and plate stacked neatly by her bed. Records kept by Washington's father show that there were about 25 slaves at Pope's Creek when Washington was a boy.

WILLIAMSBURG

Carters Grove—Rt. 60 East, eight miles southeast of Williamsburg. (804) 220-7452. Hours: daily 9-5, March-December. A plantation museum that illustrates the difference between the life of the city and the country slave. Part of the Williamsburg restoration, Carters Grove includes a colonial mansion furnished with antiques, slave cabins, and tours of the property directed by costumed interpreters.

Colonial Williamsburg—in the historic district of Williamsburg, (804) 220-7645. Hours: daily 9-5. The former capitol city of Virginia, Colonial Williamsburg contains over 80 restored eighteenth-century buildings. Historic exhibits include dramatic productions of slave life, African-American music programs, story-telling, and a two-hour walking tour of black Williamsburg.

Index

Index of Cities

Index

Index of Sites

Other Ethnic Heritage Guides Available
from Hippocrene Books:

BL

BL

BL

HI
ones

PC
USA
zak

F
B

h

s)